Principa

John Cairns

Alpha Editions

This edition published in 2024

ISBN 9789362519245

Design and Setting By
Alpha Editions
www.alphaedis.com
Email - info@alphaedis.com

Contents

PREFACE

In preparing the following pages I have been chiefly indebted for the materials of the earlier chapters to some MS. notes by my late uncle, Mr. William Cairns. These were originally written for Professor MacEwen when he was preparing his admirable *Life and Letters of John Cairns, D.D. LL.D.* They are very full and very interesting, and I have made free use of them.

To Dr. MacEwen's book I cannot sufficiently express my obligations. He has put so much relating to Principal Cairns into an absolutely final form, that he seems to have left no alternative to those who come after him between passing over in silence what he has so well said and reproducing it almost in his words. It is probable, therefore, that students of the *Life and Letters*—and there are many who, like Mr. Andrew Lang with Lockhart's *Life of Scott*, "make it their breviary "—will detect some echoes of its sentences in this little book. Still, I have tried to look at the subject from my own point of view, and to work it out in my own way; while, if I have borrowed anything directly, I trust that I have made due acknowledgment in the proper place.

Among those whom I have to thank for kind assistance, I desire specially to mention my father, the Rev. David Cairns, the last surviving member of the household at Dunglass, who has taken a constant interest in the progress of the book, and has supplied me with many reminiscences and suggestions. To my brother the Rev. D.S. Cairns, Ayton, I am indebted for most valuable help in regard to many points, especially that dealt with at the close of Chapter VI.; and I also owe much to the suggestions of my friends the Rev. P. Wilson and the Rev. R. Glaister. For help in revising the proofs I have to thank the Rev. J.M. Connor and my brother the Rev. W.T. Cairns.

J.C.

DUMFRIES, *20th March* 1903.

CHAPTER I

ANCESTRY AND CHILDHOOD

John Cairns was born at Ayton Hill, in the parish of Ayton, in the east of Berwickshire, on the 23rd of August 1818.

The farm of Ayton Hill no longer exists. Nothing is left of it but the trees which once overshadowed its buildings, and the rank growth of nettles which marks the site of a vanished habitation of man. Its position was a striking one, perched as it was just on the edge of the high ground which separates the valley of the little river Eye from that of the Tweed. It commanded an extensive view, taking in almost the whole course of the Eye, from its cradle away to the left among the Lammermoors to where it falls into the sea at Eyemouth a few miles to the right. Down in the valley, directly opposite, were the woods and mansion of Ayton Castle. A little to the left, the village of Ayton lay extended along the farther bank of the stream, while behind both castle and village the ground rose in gentle undulations to the uplands of Coldingham Moor.

South-eastwards, a few miles along the coast, lay Berwick-on-Tweed, the scene of John Cairns's future labours as a minister; while away in the opposite direction, in the heart of the Lammermoors, near the headwaters of the Whitadder and the Dye, was the home of his immediate ancestors. These were tenants of large sheep-farms; but, through adverse circumstances, his grandfather, Thomas Cairns, unable to take a farm of his own, had to earn his living as a shepherd. He died in 1799, worn out before he had passed his prime, and his widow was left to bring up her young fatherless family of three girls and two boys as best she could. After several migrations, which gradually brought them down from the hills to the seaboard, they settled for some years at Ayton Hill. The farm was at the time under some kind of trust, and there was no resident farmer. The widowed mother was engaged to look after the pigs and the poultry; the daughters also found employment; and James, the elder son, became the shepherd. He was of an adventurous and somewhat restless disposition, and, at the time of the threatened invasion by Napoleon, joined a local Volunteer corps. Then the war fever laid hold of him, and he enlisted in the regular army, serving in the Rifle Brigade all through the Peninsular War, from Vimiera to Toulouse, and earning a medal with twelve clasps. He afterwards returned, bringing with him a Portuguese wife, and settled as shepherd on the home-farm of Ayton Castle.

The younger son, John, as yet little more than a child, was hired out as herd-boy on the neighbouring farm of Greystonelees, between Ayton and Berwick. His wages were a pair of shoes in the half-year, with his food in the farm kitchen and his bed in the stable loft. His schooldays had begun early. He used afterwards to tell how his mother, when he was not more than five years old, carried him every day on her back on his way to school across a little stream that flowed near their cottage. But this early education was often interrupted, and came very soon to a close; not, however, before he was well able to read. Writing he taught himself later; and, later still, he picked up a good working knowledge of arithmetic at a night-school. He was a quiet, thoughtful boy, specially fond of reading, but, from lack of books, reading was almost out of his reach. He had not even a Bible of his own, for Bibles were then so dear that it was not possible for parents in humble life to provide those of their children who went out into the world with copies even of the cheapest sort. In place of a Bible, however, his mother had given him a copy of the Scottish Metre Version of the Psalms, with a "Preface" to each Psalm and notes by John Brown of Haddington. This was all the boy had to feed his soul on, but it was enough, for it was strong meat; and he valued and carefully kept that old, brown, leather-bound Psalm-book to the end of his days.

When James left home, the shepherding at Ayton Hill was taken up by his brother John. Though only a lad in his teens, he was in every respect, except in physical strength, already a man. He was steady and thoughtful, handy and capable in farm work, especially in all that concerned the care of sheep, for which he had a natural and probably an inherited instinct. He was also held in great regard by the Rev. David Ure, the earnest and kindly minister of the Burgher Meeting-house, which stood behind the Castle woods at the lower end of Ayton village. The family were of that "strict, not strictest species of Presbyterian Dissenter," and John attended also the Bible-class and Fellowship Meeting. The family of John Murray, a ploughman or "hind" from the Duns district, and now settled at Bastleridge, the next farm to Ayton Hill, also attended Mr. Ure's church. An intimacy sprang up between the two families. It ripened into affection between John Cairns and Alison, John Murray's only daughter, and in June 1814 they were united in marriage. The two eldest daughters of the Cairns family had already gone to situations, and were soon to have homes of their own. The grand old mother, who had been for so many years both father and mother to her children, was beginning to feel the infirmities of age. When, therefore, the young couple took up housekeeping, she left the home and the work at Ayton Hill to them, and with her youngest daughter went over to live in Ayton.

John Cairns and his wife were in many respects very unlike one another. He was of a grave, quiet, and somewhat anxious temperament, almost morbidly scrupulous where matters of conscience and responsibility were concerned. She, on the other hand, was always hopeful, making light of practical difficulties, and by her untiring energy largely helping to make these disappear. She had a great command of vigorous Scotch, and a large stock of homely proverbs, of which she made frequent and apposite use. Both husband and wife were excellently well read in their Bibles, and both were united in the fear of God. Built on this firm foundation, their union of twenty-seven years was a singularly happy one, and their different temperaments contributed to the common stock what each of them separately lacked. Ayton Hill remained their home for six years after their marriage, and here were born their three eldest children, of whom the youngest, John, is the subject of the present sketch.

In the spring of 1820 the trust under which Ayton Hill had been worked for so many years was wound up, and a new tenant took the farm. It became necessary, therefore, for the shepherd to seek a new situation, and this brought about the first "flitting" in the family history. The Berwickshire hinds are somewhat notorious for their migratory habits, in which some observers have found a survival of the restlessness which characterised their ancestors in former times, and was alike the result and the cause of the old Border Forays. Be that as it may, every Whitsunday term-day sees the country roads thronged with carts conveying furniture and bedding from one farm to another. In front of the pile sits the hind's wife with her younger children, while the hind himself with his older boys and girls walks beside the horse, or brings up the rear, driving the family cow before him. In some cases there is a flitting every year, and instances have even been known in which anxiety to preserve an unbroken tradition of annual removals has been satisfied by a flitting from one house to another on the same farm.

The Cairns family now entered on a period of migration of this kind, and in the course of eleven years they flitted no less than six times. Their first removal was from Ayton Hill to Oldcambus Mains, in the parish of Cockburnspath, where they came into touch with the Dunglass estate and the Stockbridge Church, with both of which they were in after-years to have so close a connection. The father had been engaged by the Dunglass factor to act, in the absence of a regular tenant, as joint steward and shepherd at Oldcambus, and the family lived in the otherwise unoccupied farmhouse. The two elder children attended a school less than a mile distant, and in their absence John, the youngest, who was now in his fourth year, used to cause no little anxiety to his careful mother by wandering out by himself dangerously near to the edge of the high sea-cliffs behind the farmhouse.

At length, in a happy moment, he took it into his head to go to school himself; and, although he was too young for lessons, the schoolmaster allowed him to sit beside his brother and sister. When he was tired of sitting, tradition has it that the little fellow used to amuse himself by getting up and standing in the corner to which the school culprits were sent. Here he duly put on the dunce's cap which he had seen them wear, and which bore the inscription, "For my bad conduct I stand here."

A tenant having been at length found for Oldcambus Mains, the family, which had been increased by the birth of three more children, removed back to the Ayton district, to the farm of Whiterigg, two miles from the village. The house which they occupied here is still pointed out, but it has been enlarged and improved since those days. At that time, like all the farm servants' dwellings in the district, it consisted of a single room with an earthen floor, an open unlined roof of red tiles, and rafters running across and resting on the wall at each side. There was a fireplace at one end and a window, and then a door at right angles to the fireplace. When the furniture came to be put in, the two box-beds with their sliding panels were set up facing the fireplace; they touched the back wall at one end, and left a small space free opposite to the door at the other. The beds came almost, if not quite, up to the level of the rafters, and screened off behind them perhaps a third of the entire space, which was used as a lumber closet or store. Above the rafters, well furnished with *cleeks* for the family stock of hams, there was spread, in lieu of a ceiling, a large sheet of canvas or coarse unbleached cotton. There was a table under the window, a *dresser* with racks for plates, etc., set up against the opposite wall, and an eight-day clock between the window and the fireplace. "Fixtures" were in such houses practically non-existent; the grate, which consisted merely of two or three bars or *ribs*, the iron *swey* from which hung the large pot with its rudimentary feet, and, in some cases, even the window, were the property of the immigrants, and were carried about by them from farm to farm in their successive flirtings.

When at Whiterigg, the children attended school at Ayton, and here young John learned his letters and made considerable progress in reading. After two years, the death of the Whiterigg farmer made another change necessary, and the family returned to the Dunglass estate and settled at Aikieside, a forester's cottage quite near to their former home at Oldcambus Mains, and within easy reach of Oldcambus School. Aikieside is in the Pease Dean, a magnificent wooded glen, crossed a little lower down by a famous bridge which carries the old post road from Edinburgh to Berwick over the Pease Burn at a height of nearly one hundred and thirty feet. A still older road crosses the stream close to its mouth, less than a mile below the bridge. The descent here is very steep on both sides, but it seems to have been even steeper in former times than it is now. This point in the old road is "the strait Pass at Copperspath," where Oliver Cromwell before the battle of Dunbar found the way to Berwick blocked by the troops of General Leslie, and of which he said that here "ten men to hinder are better than forty to make their way."

Beautiful as the Pease Dean is, it has this drawback for those who live in the vicinity—especially if they happen to be anxious mothers—that it is infested with adders; and as these engaging reptiles were specially numerous and specially aggressive in the "dry year" 1826, it is not surprising that when, owing to the cottage at Aikieside being otherwise required, John Cairns was offered a house in the village of Cockburnspath, he and his wife gladly availed themselves of that offer. From Cockburnspath another removal was made in the following year to Dunglass Mill; and at last, in 1831, the much travelled family, now increased to eight, found rest in a house within the Dunglass grounds, after the father had received the appointment of shepherd on the home-farm, which he held during the rest of his life.

CHAPTER II

DUNGLASS

The Lammermoor range, that "dusky continent of barren heath-hills," as Thomas Carlyle calls it, runs down into the sea at St. Abb's Head. For the greater part of its length it divides Berwickshire from East Lothian; but at its seaward end there is one Berwickshire parish lying to the north of it— the parish of Cockburnspath. The land in this parish slopes down to the Firth of Forth; it is rich and well cultivated, and is divided into large farms, each of which has its group of red-roofed buildings, its substantial farmhouse, and its long tail of hinds' cottages. The seaward views are very fine, and include the whole of the rugged line of coast from Fast Castle on the east to Tantallon and North Berwick Law on the west. In the middle distance are the tower of Dunbar Church, the Bass Rock, and the Isle of May; and farther off is the coast of Fife, with Largo Law and the Lomonds in the background. The land is mostly bare of trees, but there is a notable exception to this in the profound ravines which come down from the hills to the sea, and whose banks are thickly clothed with fine natural wood.

Of these, the Pease Dean has already been mentioned. Close beside it is the Tower Dean, so called from an ancient fortalice of the Home family which once defended it, and which stands beside a bridge held in just execration by all cyclists on the Great North Road. But, unquestionably, the finest of all the ravines in these parts is Dunglass Dean, which forms the western boundary of Cockburnspath parish, and divides Berwickshire from East Lothian. From the bridge by which the Edinburgh and Berwick road crosses the dean, at the height of one hundred feet above the bed of the stream, the view in both directions is extremely fine. About a hundred and fifty yards lower down is the modern railway bridge, which spans the ravine in one gigantic arch forty feet higher than the older structure that carries the road; and through this arch, above the trees which fill the glen, one gets a beautiful glimpse of the sea about half a mile away.

Above the road-bridge, and to the right of the wooded dean, are the noble trees and parks of Dunglass grounds. The mansion-house, a handsome modern building, part of which rises to a height of five storeys, is built only some eight or ten feet from the brink of the dean, on its western or East Lothian side. About fifty yards farther west are the ivy-covered ruins of a fine Gothic church, whose massive square tower and stone roof are still tolerably complete. This church before the Reformation had collegiate rank, and is now the sole remaining relic of the ancient village of

Dunglass. In former times the Dunglass estate belonged to the Earls of Home, whose second title, borne to this day by the eldest son of the house, is that of Lord Dunglass. But it was bought about the middle of the seventeenth century by the Halls, who own it still, and in whose family there has been a baronetcy since 1687. The laird at the time with which we are now dealing was Sir James Hall, whose epitaph in the old church at Dunglass bears that he was "a philosopher eminent among the distinguished men of an enquiring age." He was President of the Royal Society of Edinburgh for many years, and was an acknowledged expert in Natural Science, especially in Geology. His second son was the well-known Captain Basil Hall, R.N., the author of a once widely-read book of travels.

Behind the church, and about a hundred yards to the west of the mansion-house, are the offices—stables, close boxes, coach-house, etc., all of a single storey, and built round a square paved courtyard. The coachman's house is on one side of this square, and the shepherd's on the other. The latter, which is on the side farthest from the "big house," has its back to the courtyard, and looks out across a road to its little bailyard and a fine bank of trees beyond it. It is neat and lightsome, but very small; consisting only of a single room thirteen feet by twelve, with a closet opening off it not more than six feet broad. How a family consisting of a father, mother, and eight children could be stowed away in it, especially at night, is rather a puzzling question. But we may suppose that, when all were at home, each of the two box-beds would be made to hold three, that a smaller bed in the closet would account for two more, and that for the accommodation of two of the younger children a sliding shelf would be inserted transversely across the foot of one of the box-beds. Certainly, an arrangement of this kind would fail to be approved by a sanitary inspector in our times; and even during the day, when all the family were on the floor together, there was manifest overcrowding. But the life was a country one, and could be, and was, largely spent in the open air, amid healthful surroundings and beautiful scenery.

The income available for the support of such a large household seems to us in these days almost absurdly inadequate. The father's wages rarely exceeded £30 a year, and they never all his life reached £40. They were mostly paid in kind. So many bolls of oats, of barley and of peas, so many carts of coals, so many yards of growing potatoes, a cow's grass, the keep of two sheep and as many pigs, and a free house,—these, which were known as the *gains*, were the main items in the account. This system gave considerable opportunity for management on the part of a thrifty housewife, and for such management there were few to surpass the housewife in the shepherd's cottage at Dunglass.

The food was plentiful but plain. Breakfast consisted of porridge and milk; dinner, in the middle of the day, of Scotch kail and pork, occasionally varied by herrings, fresh or salt according to the season, and with the usual accompaniments of potatoes and pease bannocks. At supper there was porridge again, or mashed potatoes washed down with draughts of milk, and often eaten with horn spoons out of the large pot which was set down on the hearth. Tea was only seen once a week—on Sunday afternoons. And so the young family grew up healthy and strong in spite of the overcrowding.

Before the removal to Dunglass, the two eldest children had been taken from school to work in the fields, where they earned wages beginning at sixpence a day. Their education, however, was continued in some sort at a night-school. John and his younger brother James, and the twins, Janet and William, who came next in order, attended the parish school at Cockburnspath, a mile away. Cockburnspath is a village of about two hundred and fifty inhabitants, situated a little off the main road. It has a church with an ancient round tower, and a venerable market-cross rising from a platform of steps in the middle of the village street.

On the south side of the street, just in front of the church, stood the old schoolhouse—a low one storey building, roofed with the red tiles characteristic of the neighbourhood, and built on to the schoolmaster's two-storey dwelling. The schoolmaster at this time was John M'Gregor, a man of ripe and accurate scholarship and quite separate individuality. The son of a Perthshire farmer, he had studied for the ministry at St. Andrews University, and had, it was said, fulfilled all the requirements for becoming a licentiate of the Church of Scotland except the sending in of one exercise. This exercise he could never be persuaded to send in, and that not because he had any speculative difficulties as to the truth of the Christian revelation, nor yet because he had any exaggerated misgivings as to his own qualifications for the work of the ministry; but because he preferred the teaching profession, and was, moreover, indignant at what he conceived to be the overbearing attitude which the ministers of the Established Church assumed to the parish schools and schoolmasters. This feeling ultimately became a kind of mania with him. He was at feud with his own parish minister, and never entered his church except when, arrayed in a blue cloak with a red collar, he attended to read proclamations of marriages; and he could make himself very disagreeable when the local Presbytery sent their annual deputation to examine his school. Yet he was essentially a religious man; he had a reverence for what was good, and he taught the Bible and Shorter Catechism to his scholars carefully and well.

As he disliked the ministers, so he showed little deference to the farmers, who were in some sort the "quality" of the district, and to such of their offspring as came under his care. The farmers retaliated by setting up an opposition school in Cockburnspath, which survived for a few years; but it never flourished, for the common people believed in M'Gregor, whom they regarded as "a grand teacher," as indeed he was. He had a spare, active figure, wore spectacles, and took snuff. There was at all times an element of grimness in him, and he could be merciless when the occasion seemed to demand it. "Stark man he was, and great awe men had of him," but this awe had its roots in a very genuine respect for his absolutely just dealing and his masterful independence of character.

John Cairns first went to Mr. M'Gregor's school when the family removed to Cockburnspath from Aikieside, and he made such progress that two years later, when he was ten years old, the master proposed that he should join a Latin class which was then being formed. This proposal caused great searchings of heart at home. His father, with anxious conscientiousness, debated with himself as to whether it would be right for him thus to set one of his sons above the rest. He could not afford to have them all taught Latin, so would it be fair to the others that John should be thus singled out from them? The mother, on the other hand, had no such misgivings, and she was clear that John must have his Latin. The ordinary school fees ranged from three to five shillings a quarter; but when Latin was taken they rose to seven and sixpence. Mr. M'Gregor had proposed to teach John Latin without extra charge, but both his father and his mother were agreed that to accept this kind offer was not to be thought of for a moment; and his mother was sure that by a little contriving and saving on her part the extra sum could be secured. The minister, Mr. Inglis, who was consulted in the matter, also pronounced strongly for the proposal, and so John was allowed to begin his classical studies.

Within two years Greek had been added to the Latin; and, as the unavoidable bustle and noise which arose in the evening when the whole family were together in the one room of the house made study difficult, John stipulated with his mother that she should call him in the morning, when she rose, an hour before anybody else, to light the fire and prepare the breakfast. And so it happened that, if any of the rest of the family awoke before it was time to get up, they would see John studying his lesson and hear him conjugating his Greek verbs by the light of the one little oil-lamp that the house afforded. Perhaps, too, it was what he saw, in these early morning hours, of the unwearied and self-forgetful toil of his mother that taught him to be in an especial degree thoughtful for her comfort and considerate of her wants both then and in after-years.

But his regular schooldays were now drawing to an end. His father, though engaged as the shepherd at Dunglass, had other duties of a very multifarious kind to discharge, and part of his shepherd work had been done for him for some time by his eldest son, Thomas. But Thomas was now old enough to earn a higher wage by other work on the home-farm or in the woods, and so it came to be John's turn to take up the work among the sheep. When his father told Mr. M'Gregor that John would have to leave school, the schoolmaster was so moved with regret at the thought of losing so promising a scholar, that he said that if John could find time for any study during the day he would be glad to have him come to his house two or three nights in the week, and to go over with him then what he had learned. As Mr. M'Gregor had become more and more solitary in his habits of late—he was a bachelor, and his aged mother kept house for him—this offer was considered to be a very remarkable proof of his regard, and it was all the more gratefully accepted on that account.

It fortunately happened that the work to which John had now to turn his hand allowed him an opportunity of carrying on his studies without interfering with its efficiency. That work was of a twofold character. He had to "look" the sheep, and he had to "herd" them. The looking came first. Starting at six o'clock in the morning, accompanied by the faithful collie "Cheviot," he made a round of all the grass-parks on the home-farm, beginning down near the sea and thence working his way round to a point considerably higher up than the mansion-house. His instructions were to count the sheep in each field, so that he might be able to tell whether they were all there, and also to see whether they were all afoot and feeding. In the event of anything being wrong, he was to report it to his father. The circuit was one of three or four miles, and the last field to be looked was that in which were gathered the fifty or sixty sheep that were to be brought out to the unfenced lawns round the mansion-house and be herded there during the day.

These sheep were generally to be found waiting close to the gate, and when it was opened they could quite easily find their own way down to their feeding-ground. As they passed slowly on, cropping the grass as they went, John was able to leave them and go home for his breakfast of porridge and milk. Breakfast having been despatched, and Cheviot fed, he once more wrapped his shepherd's plaid about him, remembering to put a book or two, and perhaps a piece of bannock, into the *neuk* of it, and set out to find his flock. There was usually little difficulty in doing so, for the sheep knew the way and did not readily wander out of it; while, even if they had deviated a little from the direct route, no great harm would at this stage of their passage have resulted. It was quite different when they came down to the lawns near the house. These were surrounded by ornamental shrubbery, and it was to keep the sheep from invading this and the adjacent flower-borders that the services of the herd-boy were required.

What he had to do, then, after he had brought the sheep down, was to take his place on some knoll which commanded the ground where they were feeding, and keep an eye on them. If nothing disturbed them they would feed quietly enough, and a long spell of reading might be quite safely indulged in. If any of them showed signs of wandering out of bounds, a stroll in their direction, book in hand, would usually be quite sufficient, with or without Cheviot's aid, to turn them. And if a leading sheep were turned, the others would, sheep-like, follow the new lead thus imparted. This was the usual state of things in fine weather. In wet weather there were not the same possibilities of study, unless the feeding-ground happened to be in the neighbourhood of the old church, where sufficient shelter could be found for reading and the sheep could be watched through the open doorway. About four o'clock—in winter somewhat earlier—it was time to take the sheep back to the fold-field, and then the parks had to be again looked, this time in the reverse order, the shepherd's cottage being gained in time for supper.

After supper, John would go into Cockburnspath to recite the lessons he had prepared to Mr. M'Gregor. The schoolmaster never prescribed any definite section to be learned; he left this to his pupil, in whose industry and interest in his work he had sufficient confidence. He rarely bestowed any praise. A grim smile of satisfaction, and sometimes a "Very well, sir," were all that he would vouchsafe; but to others he would be less reticent, and once he was heard to say, "I have so far missed my own way, but John Cairns will flourish yet."

John is described as having been at this time a well-grown boy, somewhat raw-boned and loose-jointed, with an eager look, ruddy and healthy, and tanned with the sun, his hair less dark than it afterwards became. He was fond of schoolboy games—shinty, football, and the rest—and would play at marbles, even when the game went against him, until he had lost his last stake. Archery was another favourite amusement, and he was expert at making bows from the thinnings of the Dunglass yews, and arrows tipped with iron *ousels*—almost the only manual dexterity he possessed. Like all boys of his class, his usual dress was a brown velveteen jacket and waistcoat and corduroy trousers that had once been white.

Along with the teaching he got from Mr. M'Gregor, there went another sort of education of a less formal kind which still deserves to be mentioned. Now that he was earning a wage,—it was about eightpence or tenpence a day,—which of course went into the common stock, he ventured occasionally to ask his mother for sixpence to himself. With this he could obtain a month's reading at the Cockburnspath library. A very excellent library this was, and during the three years of his herding he worked his way pretty well through it. It was especially strong in history and standard theology, and in these departments included such works as Gibbon's *Decline and Fall*, Mitford's *History of Greece*, Russell's *Modern Europe*, Butler's *Analogy*, and Paley's *Evidences*. In biography and fiction it was less strong, but it had a complete set of the Waverley Novels in one of the early three-volume editions. When he went to Mr. M'Gregor's, John used often to take butter churned by his mother to the village shop, and the basket in which he carried it was capacious enough to hold a good load of books from the library on the return journey.

All the family were fond of books, and the small store of volumes, mostly of old Scotch divinity, in the little bookcase at Dunglass was well thumbed. But reading of a lighter kind was also indulged in, and on winter nights, when the mother was plying her spinning-wheel and the father had taken down his cobbler's box and was busily engaged patching the children's shoes, it was a regular practice for John to sit near the dim oil-lamp and read to the rest. Sometimes the reading would be from an early number of Chambers's *Journal*, sometimes from Wilson's *Tales of the Borders*, which were then appearing—both of these being loans from a neighbour. But once a week there was always a newspaper to be read. It was often a week or a fortnight old, for, as it cost sixpence halfpenny, it was only by six or eight neighbours clubbing together that such a luxury could be brought within the reach of a working-man's family; but it was never so old as to be uninteresting to such eager listeners.

But the most powerful of all the influences which affected John Cairns at this period of his life remains to be mentioned—that which came to him from his religious training and surroundings. The Christian religion has acted both directly and indirectly on the Scottish peasantry, and it has done so the more powerfully because of the democratic character of the Presbyterian form which that religion took in Scotland. Directly, it has changed their lives and has given them new motives and new immortal hopes. But it has also acted on them indirectly, doing for them in this respect much of what education and culture have done for others. It has supplied the element of idealism in their lives. These lives, otherwise commonplace and unlovely, have been lighted up by a perpetual vision of the unseen and the eternal; and this has stimulated their intellectual powers and has so widened their whole outlook upon life as to raise them high above those of their own class who lived only for the present. All who have listened to the prayers of a devout Scotch elder of the working-class must have been struck by this combination of spiritual and intellectual power; and one thing they must have specially noticed is that, unlike the elder of contemporary fiction, he expressed himself, not in broad Scotch but in correct and often stately Bible English.

But this intellectual activity is often carried beyond the man in whom it has first manifested itself. It tends to reappear in his children, who either inherit it or have their own intellectual powers stimulated in the bracing atmosphere it has created. The instances of Robert Burns and Thomas Carlyle, who both came out of homes in which religion—and religion of the old Scottish type—was the deepest interest, will occur to everyone. Not the least striking illustration of this principle is shown in the case of John Cairns. In the life of his soul he owed much to the godly upbringing and Christian example shown to him by his parents; but the home at Dunglass, where religion was always the chief concern, was the nursery of a strong mind as well as of a strong soul, and both were fed from the same spring. In this case, as in so many others, spiritual strength became intellectual strength in the second generation.

The Cairns family attended church at Stockbridge, a mile beyond Cockburnspath and two miles from Dunglass, and the father was an elder there from 1831 till his death. The United Secession—formerly the Burgher—Church at Stockbridge occupied a site conveniently central for the wide district which it served, but very solitary. It stood amid cornfields, on the banks of a little stream, and looked across to the fern-clad slopes of Ewieside, an outlying spur of the Lammermoors. Except the manse, and the beadle's cottage which adjoined it, there was no house within sight, nor any out of sight less than half a mile away.

The minister at this time was the Rev. David M'Quater Inglis, a man of rugged appearance and of original and vigorous mental powers. He was a good scholar and a stimulating preacher, excelling more particularly in his expository discourses, or "lectures" as they used to be called. When he tackled some intricate passage in an Epistle, it was at times a little hard to follow him, especially as his utterance tended to be hesitating; but when he had finished, one saw that a broad clear road had been cut through the thicket, and that the daylight had been let in upon what before had been dim. "I have heard many preachers," said Dr. Cairns, in preaching his funeral sermon nearly forty years later, "but I have heard few whose sermons at their best were better than the best of his; and his everyday ones had a strength, a simplicity, and an unaffected earnestness which excited both thought and Christian feeling." Nor was he merely a preacher. By his pastoral visitations and "diets of examination" he always kept himself in close touch with his people, and he made himself respected by rich and poor alike.

The shepherd's family occupied a pew at Stockbridge in front of the pulpit and just under the gallery, which ran round three sides of the church. That pew was rarely vacant on a Sunday. There was no herding to be done on that day, and in the morning the father looked the sheep in the parks himself that the herd-boy might have his full Sabbath rest. He came back in time to conduct family worship, this being the only morning in the week when it was possible for him to do so, although in the evening it was never omitted, and on Sunday evening was always preceded by a repetition of the Shorter Catechism. After worship the family set out for church, where the service began at eleven.

The situation of Stockbridge, it has been already said, was solitary, but on Sundays, when the hour of worship drew near, the place lost its solitude. The roads in all directions were thronged with vehicles, men on horseback, and a great company on foot; the women wearing the scarlet cloaks which had not yet given place to the Paisley shawls of a later period, and each carrying, neatly wrapped in a white handkerchief, a Bible or Psalm-book, between whose leaves were a sprig or two of southernwood, spearmint, or other fragrant herb from the cottage garden.

The service lasted about three hours. There was first a "lecture" and then a sermon, each about fifty minutes long; several portions of psalms were sung; and of the three prayers, the first, or "long prayer," was seldom less than twenty minutes in length. In summer there was an interval of half an hour between the lecture and the sermon, "when," says Mr. William Cairns, "there was opportunity for a delightful breathing-time, and the youths who were swift of foot could just reach the bottom of a hill whereon were plenteous blaeberries, and snatch a fearful joy if one could swallow without leaving the tell-tale marks on the lips and tongue."

At the close of the afternoon service there was a Sunday school, chiefly conducted by Mr. Inglis himself, at which an examination on the sermon that had just been delivered formed an important part of the exercises. And tradition has it that the questioning and answering, which had at first been evenly distributed among the pupils, usually in the end came to resolve themselves pretty much into a dialogue between Mr. Inglis and John Cairns. It was here that the minister first came to close grips with his elder's son and took the measure of the lad's abilities. After he did so, his interest in John's classical studies was constant and helpful; and, although he gave him no direct assistance in them (if he had done so, he would have called down upon himself the wrath of Mr. M'Gregor), he was always ready to lend him books and give him useful advice.

After three years at herding and at Mr. M'Gregor's, the question arose, and was the subject of anxious debate in the family councils, as to what was to be done with John. He was now sixteen. His elder brother, Thomas, had got a post under his father, whom he afterwards succeeded as shepherd at Dunglass. His elder sister had gone to a situation. And now James, the brother next younger than himself, had also left home to be apprenticed to a tailor. It was time for some decision to be come to with regard to him. Mr. M'Gregor was anxious that a superstructure should be built on the foundation laid by himself by his going to College. Mr. Inglis's advice was unhesitatingly given in the same direction. With his father, the old scruples arose about setting one of his children above the rest; but again his mother's chief concern was more about ways and means. His father's question was, *Ought* it to be done? his mother's, *Can* it be done? There were great difficulties in the way of answering this practical question in the affirmative. There were then no bursaries open for competition; and though the expenses at home were not so great as they had once been, now that three of the family had been so far placed in life, the University class-fees and the cost of living, even in the most frugal way, entailed an expense which was formidable enough. Still, the mother thought that this could be faced, and, in order to acquaint herself more fully with all the facts of the situation, she resolved to pay a long-promised visit to her youngest brother, who with his family was now living in Edinburgh. He was a carrier between that city and Jedburgh, and, though still in a comparatively humble way, was said to be doing well.

The visit was a great success. Mrs. Cairns was most warmly received by her brother and his wife, who proposed that John should stay with them and share with their own family in what was going. This offer was gratefully accepted, so far as the question of lodging was concerned. As to board, John's mother had ideas of her own, and insisted on paying for it, if not in money at least in kind. Thus it was settled that John was to go to College, but nothing was settled beyond this. Perhaps his parents may have had their own wishes, and his minister and his schoolmaster their own expectations, about a career for him; but in the boy's unworldly heart there was nothing as yet beyond the desire for further learning and the earnest resolution to be not unworthy of the sacrifices which had made the realisation of this desire possible. He worked at his herding up till the day before he left for the University, in the end of October 1834; and then, starting in the middle of the night with William Christison, the Cockburnspath carrier, he trudged beside the cart that conveyed the box containing his clothes and his scanty stock of books all the thirty-five miles between Dunglass and Edinburgh.

CHAPTER III

COLLEGE DAYS

When John Cairns entered the University of Edinburgh in November 1834 he passed into a world that was entirely strange to him. It would be difficult to imagine a greater contrast than that between the low-roofed village school and the spacious quadrangle surrounded by heavily balustraded stone terraces and stately pillared façades, into which, at the booming of the hourly bell, there poured from the various classrooms a multitudinous throng of eager young humanity. And he himself in some mysterious way seemed to be changed almost beyond his own recognition. Instead of being the Jock Cairns who had herded sheep on the braes of Dunglass, and had carried butter to the Cockburnspath shop, he was now, as his matriculation card informed him, "Joannes Cairns, Civis Academiae Edinburgeniae;" he was addressed by the professor in class as "Mr. Cairns," and was included in his appeal to "any gentleman in the bench" to elucidate a difficult passage in the lesson of the day.

He attended two classes this winter—that of "Humanity" or Latin taught by Professor Pillans, and that of Greek under the care of Professor George Dunbar. Pillans had been a master at Eton, and at a later period Rector of the Edinburgh High School. He was a little man with rosy cheeks, and was a sound scholar and an admirable teacher, whose special "fad" was Classical Geography. Dunbar had begun life as a working gardener at Ayton Castle. He had compiled a Greek Lexicon which had some repute in its day, but he was not an inspiring teacher, and his gruff manners made him far from popular.

Trained by a country schoolmaster, and having no experience of competition except what a country school affords, John Cairns had until now no idea of his own proficiency relatively to that of others; and it was something of a revelation to him when he discovered how far the grounding he had received from Mr. M'Gregor enabled him to go. His classical attainments soon attracted notice, and at the end of the session, although he failed to win the Class Medals, he stood high in the Honours Lists, and was first in private Latin studies and in Greek prose. Nor were these the only interests that occupied him. A fellow-student, the late Dr. James Hardy, writes of him that from the first he was great in controversy, and that in the classroom during the ten minutes before the appearance of the professor, he was always the centre of a knot of disputants on the Voluntary Church question or some question of politics. Also it is recorded that, on the day after a Parliamentary election for the city, he had no voice left, having shouted it all away the day before in honour of the two successful Whig candidates.

During this session, as had been previously arranged, he lodged in Charles Street with his mother's brother, whose eldest son, John Murray, shared his room. For this cousin, who was about his own age, he had always the greatest regard, and he was specially grateful to him for the kindness with which he helped him over many of the difficulties which, as a raw lad from the country, he experienced when he first came to live in the city. The friendship between the cousins remained unbroken—though their paths in life were widely different—till they died, within a fortnight of each other, nearly sixty years later.

All through the winter a box travelled with the Cockburnspath carrier every three or four weeks between Edinburgh and Dunglass, taking with it on the outward journey clothes to be washed and mended, and on the return journey always including a store of country provisions—scones, oatmeal, butter, cheese, bacon, and potatoes. The letters that passed between the student and his family were also sent in the box, for as yet there was no penny post, and the postage of a letter between Dunglass and Edinburgh cost as much as sixpence halfpenny or sevenpence. Often, too, John would send home some cheap second-hand books, for he had a general commission to keep his eye on the bookstalls. Amongst these purchases was sometimes included a Bible, so that before the end of the winter each member of the family had a separate Bible to take to church or Sunday school.

At the close of the winter session he accepted the invitation of another brother of his mother, who was a farmer at Longyester, near Gifford in East Lothian, on the northern fringe of the Lammermoors, to come and be tutor to his three boys during the summer. At Longyester he spent four very happy months in congenial work among kind people. He learned to ride, and more than once he rode along the hill-foots to Dunglass, twenty miles to the eastward, to spend the Sunday with his father and mother.

During these months he also came into personal contact with a family whose influence on him during these early years was strong and memorable—the Darlings of Millknowe. Millknowe is a large sheep-farm in the heart of the Lammermoors, just where the young Whitadder winds round the base of Spartleton Law. The family at Millknowe, consisting at this time of three brothers and two sisters, all of whom had reached middle life, were relatives of his father, the connection dating from the time when his forebears were farmers in the same region. They were a notable family, full of all kinds of interesting lore, literary, scientific, and pastoral, and they exercised a boundless hospitality to all, whether gentle or simple, who came within their reach. One of them, a maiden sister, Miss Jean Darling, took a special charge of her young cousin, and in a special degree won his confidence. From the first she understood him. She saw the power that was awakening within him, and was, particularly in his student days, his friend and adviser.

As the summer of 1835 advanced, it came to be a grave question with him whether he could return to college in the ensuing winter. His father had had a serious illness; and, though he was now recovering, there was a doctor's bill to settle, and he still required more care and better nourishment than ordinary. Cairns was afraid that, with these extra expenses to be met, his own return to College might involve too serious a drain on the family resources. While matters were in this state, and while he was still at Longyester, he received a request from Mr. Trotter, the schoolmaster of his native parish of Ayton, to come and assist him in the school and with the tuition of boarders in his house. This offer was quite in the line of the only ideas as to his future life he had as yet entertained; for, so far as he had thought seriously on the subject, he had thought of being a teacher. On the other hand, while his great ambition was to return to the University, the fact that most of his class-fellows in the past session had been older than himself suggested to him that he could quite well afford to delay a year before he returned.

So he went to Ayton, lodging while there with his father's youngest sister, Nancy, who had come thither from Ayton Hill along with her mother, when her brother John was married in 1814, and had remained there ever since. Cairns had not been two months in Ayton before his responsibilities were considerably increased. Mr. Trotter resigned his office, and the heritors asked the assistant to take charge of the school until a new teacher should be appointed. There were between one hundred and fifty and two hundred children in the school; he was the sole teacher, and he was only seventeen. Moreover, some delay occurred before the teacher who had been appointed to succeed Mr. Trotter could come to take up his work. But Cairns proved equal to the situation. The tradition is that his rule was an exceedingly stern one, that he kept the children hard at work, and that he flogged extensively and remorselessly.

When the new master arrived upon the scene, he subsided into his original post of assistant. It had been his original intention to go back to the University in November 1836; but as that date approached it became evident that the financial difficulty was not yet removed, so he accepted an engagement to continue his work in Ayton for another year.

His stay in Ayton was a very happy one. He liked his work, and had several warm friends in the village and district. Among these were Mr. Ure, the kindly old minister who had married his parents and baptized himself. Then there was Mr. Stark, minister of another Secession church in the village—a much younger man than Mr. Ure, but a good scholar and a well-read theologian. There was also a fellow-student, Henry Weir, whose parents lived in Berwick, and who used often to walk out to Ayton to see him, Cairns returning the visits, and seeing for the first time, under Weir's auspices, the old Border town in which so much of his own life was to be spent.

All this while he was working hard at his private studies. To these studies he gave all the time that was not taken up by his teaching. He read at his meals, and so far into the night that his aunt became alarmed for his health. He worked his way through a goodly number of the Greek and Latin classics, in copies borrowed from the libraries of the two ministers; and he not only read, but analysed and elaborately annotated what he read. But in the notes of the books read during the year 1837 a change becomes evident. It can be seen that he took more and more to the study of theology and Christian evidences, and his note-books are full of references to Baxter and Jeremy Taylor, to Robert Hall, Chalmers, and Keith.

At length in the summer a crisis was reached. A letter to his father, which has not been preserved, announced that his views and feelings with regard to spiritual things had undergone a great and far-reaching change, and that religion had become to him a matter of personal and paramount concern. Another letter to Henry Weir on the same subject is of great interest. It is written in the unformed and somewhat stilted style which he had not yet got rid of, and, with characteristic reticence, it deals only indirectly with the details of the experience through which he has passed, being in form a disquisition on the importance of personal religion, and a refutation of objections which might occur to his correspondent against making it the main interest of his life.

"My dear Henry," the letter concludes, "I most earnestly wish that you would devote the energies of your mind to the attentive consideration of religion, and I have no doubt that, through the tuition of the Divine Spirit, you would speedily arrive at the same conviction of the importance of the subject with myself, and then our friendship would, by the influence of those feelings which religion implants, be more hallowed and intimate than before. I long ardently to see you."

The experience which has thus been described caused no great rift with the past, nor did it produce any great change in his outward life. He did not dedicate himself to the ministry; he did not, so far as can be gathered, even become a member of the Church; and although for a short time he talked of concentrating his energies on the Greek Testament, to the disparagement of the Greek and Latin classical writers, within two months we find him back at his old studies and strenuously preparing for the coming session at College. But a new power had entered into his life, and that power gradually asserted itself as the chief and dominating influence there.

Cairns returned to the University in the late autumn of 1837, enrolling himself in the classes of Latin, Greek, and Logic. Although he maintained his intimacy with his uncle's family, he now went into lodgings in West Richmond Street, sharing a room with young William Inglis, son of the minister at Stockbridge, then a boy at the High School. Here is the description he gives to his parents of his surroundings and of the daily routine of his life: "The lodging which we occupy is a very good room, measuring 18 feet by 16 feet, in every way neat and comfortable. The walls are hung with pictures, and the windows adorned with flowers. The rent is 3s. 6d., with a promise of abatement when the price of coals is lowered. This is no doubt a great sum of money, but I trust it will be amply compensated by the honesty, cleanliness, economy, and good temper of the landlady.... I shall give you the details of my daily life:—Rise at 8; 8.30-10, Latin class; 10-1, private study; 1-2, Logic; 2-3, Greek class; 4-12.30, private study. As to meals—breakfast on porridge and treacle at 8.15; dine on broth and mutton, or varieties of potatoes with beef or fish, at 3.15; coffee at 7; if hungry, a little bread before bed. I can live quite easily and comfortably on 3s. or 3s. 6d. per week, and when you see me you will find that I have grown fat on students' fare."

At the close of the session he thus records the result of his work in one of the classes:—

"There is a circumstance which but for its connection with the subject of clothes I should not now mention. You are aware that a gold medal is given yearly by the Society of Writers to the Signet to the best scholar in the Latin class. Five are selected to compete for it by the votes of their fellow-students. Having been placed in the number a fortnight ago, I have, after a pretty close trial, been declared the successful competitor. The grand sequence is this, that at the end of the session I must come forward in the presence of many of the Edinburgh grandees and deliver a Latin oration as a prelude to receiving the medal. Although I have little fear that an oration will be forthcoming of the ordinary length and quality, I doubt that the trepidation of so unusual a position will cause me to break down in the delivery of it; but we shall see. The reference of this subject to the clothes you will at once discern. The trousers are too tight, and an addition must be made to their length. The coat is too wide in the body, too short and tight in the sleeves, and too spare in the skirt. As to my feelings I shall say nothing, because I do not look upon the honour as one of a kind that ought to excite the least elation ... I would not wish you to blazon it, nor would I, but for the cause mentioned, have taken any notice of it."

Besides this medal, he obtained the first place in the Greek class. In Logic he stood third, and he carried off a number of other prizes. He had been in every way the better for the interruption in his course; his powers had matured, he knew what he could do, and he was able to do it at will, and from this point onward he was recognised as easily the first man of his time in the University. But he had now to look about him for employment in the vacation; and for a while, in spite of the successes of the past session, he was unable to find it, and was glad to take some poorly paid elementary teaching. But at length, by the good offices of one of the masters in the Edinburgh Academy, backed by the strong recommendation of Professor Pillans, he became tutor in the family of Mr. John Donaldson, W.S., of whose house, 124 Princes Street, he became an inmate. "What I want," said Mr. Donaldson to the professor, "is a gentleman." "Well," replied Pillans, "I am sending you first-rate raw material; we shall see what you will make of it." He retained this situation till the close of his University course, to the entire satisfaction of his employer and his family, and with great comfort to himself—the salary being more than sufficient for his simple needs.

He had, as we have seen, attended the class of Logic during his second session; but as he was then devoting his main strength to classics, and as the subject was as yet quite unfamiliar to him, he did not fully give himself up to it nor yield to the influence of the professor, Sir William Hamilton. But during the summer, while he was at Mr. Donaldson's, in going again over the ground that he had traversed during the past session, he was led to read the works of Descartes, Bacon, and Leibnitz, with the result that mental philosophy at once became the supreme interest of his academic life, and, when the winter came round again, he yielded entirely to its spell and to that of the great man who was then its most distinguished British exponent.

The class of Hamilton's that he attended in the session of 1838-39 was that of Advanced Metaphysics. It so happened that at that time a hot controversy was going on about this very class. The Edinburgh Town Council, who were the patrons of Hamilton's chair, claimed also the right to decide as to what subjects the professor should lecture on, and pronounced Metaphysics to be "an abstruse subject, not generally considered as of any great or permanent utility." But, while this controversy was raging without, within all was calm. "We were quietly engaged"—wrote Cairns twenty years later—"in our discussions as to the existence of the external world while the storm was raging without, and only felt it to be another form of the *non-ego*; while the contrast between the singular gentleness and simplicity of our teacher in his dealings with his pupils, and his more impassioned qualities in controversy, became more remarkable."[1] Hamilton's philosophy may not now command the acceptance that once belonged to it, and that part of it which has been most influential may be put to-day to a use of which he did not dream, and of which he would not have approved, but Hamilton himself—"the black eagle of the desert," as the "Chaldee Manuscript" calls him—was a mighty force. The influence of that vehement and commanding personality on a generation of susceptible young men was deep and far-reaching. He seized and held the minds of his students until they were able to grasp what he had to give them,—until, in spite of the toil and pain it cost them, they were *made* to grasp it. And he further trained them in habits of mental discipline and intellectual integrity, which were of quite priceless value to them. "I am more indebted to you," wrote Cairns to him in 1848, "for the foundation of my intellectual habits and tastes than to any other person, and shall bear, by the will of the Almighty, the impress of your hand through any future stage of existence."

Cairns was first in Hamilton's class at the close of the session, and also first in Professor John Wilson's Moral Philosophy Class. "Of the many hundreds of students," Wilson wrote four years later, "whose career I have watched during the last twenty years, not one has given higher promise of excellence than John Cairns; his talents are of the highest order; his attainments in literature, philosophy, and science rare indeed; and his character such as to command universal respect."

This winter he joined with eight or nine of Hamilton's most distinguished students in forming the "Metaphysical Society," which met weekly for the purpose of discussing philosophical questions. In a Memoir which he afterwards wrote of John Clark, one of the founders of this Society, he thus describes the association that led to its being formed, and that was further cemented by its formation: "Willingly do I recall and linger upon these days and months, extending even to years, in which common studies of this abstract nature bound us together. It was the romance—the poetry—of speculation and friendship. All the vexed questions of the schools were attempted by our united strength, after our higher guide had set the example. The thorny wilds of logic were pleasant as an enchanted ground; its driest technicalities treasured up as unspeakably rare and precious. We stumbled on, making discoveries at every step, and had all things common. Each lesson in mental philosophy opened up some mystery of our immortal nature, and seemed to bring us nearer the horizon of absolute truth, which again receded as we advanced, and left us, like children pursuing the rainbow, to resume the chase. In truth, we had much of the character of childhood in these pursuits—light-heartedness, wonder, boundless hope, engrossment with the present, carelessness of the future. Our old world daily became new; and the real world of the multitude to us was but a shadow. It was but the outer world, the *non-ego*, standing at the mercy of speculation, waiting to be confirmed or abolished in the next debate; while the inner world, in which truth, beauty, and goodness had their eternal seat, should still survive and be all in all. The play of the intellect with these subtle and unworldly questions was to our minds as inevitable as the stages of our bodily growth. Happy was it for us that the play of affection was also active—nay, by sympathy excited to still greater liveliness; and that a higher wisdom suffered us not in all these flowery mazes to go astray."2

From indications contained in the brief Memoir from which this extract is taken, as well as from references in his correspondence, it would appear that about this time he subjected his religious beliefs to a careful scrutiny in the light cast upon them by his philosophical studies. From this process of testing and strain he emerged with his faith established on a yet firmer basis than before. One result of this experience may perhaps be found in a letter to his father, in which he tells him that he has been weighing the claims of the Christian ministry as his future calling in life. He feels the force of its incomparable attractions, but doubts whether he is fitted in elevation and maturity of character to undertake so vast a responsibility. Besides, he is painfully conscious of personal awkwardness in the common affairs of life, and unfitness for the practical management of business. And so he thinks he will take another year to think of it, during which he will complete his College course.

He spent the summer of 1839 with the Donaldson family at their country seat at Auchairn, near Ballantrae, in south Ayrshire, occupying most of his leisure hours in mathematical and physical studies in preparation for the work of the coming winter. In the session of 1839-40, his last at the University, he attended the classes of Natural Philosophy and Rhetoric, taking the first place in the latter and only just missing it in the former. He attended, besides, Sir William Hamilton's private classes, and was much at his house and in his company. In April 1841 he took his M.A. degree, coming out first in Classics and Philosophy, and being bracketed first in Mathematics. Among his fellow-students his reputation was maintained not merely by the honours he gained in the class lists, but by his prowess in the debating arena. Besides continuing his membership in the Metaphysical Society, he had also been, since the spring of 1839, a member of the Diagnostic, one of the most flourishing of the older students' debating societies. Of the Diagnostic he speedily became the life and soul, and discussed with ardour such questions as the Repeal of the Corn Laws, Vote by Ballot, and the Exclusion of Bishops from the House of Lords. One memorable debate took place on the Spiritual Independence of the Church, then the most burning of all Scottish public questions. The position of the Non-Intrusion party in the Established Church was maintained by Cairns's friend Clark, while he himself led on the Voluntary side. The debate lasted two nights, and, to quote the words of one who was present, "Cairns in reply swept all before him, winning a vote from those who had come in curiosity, and securing a large Liberal majority. Amidst a scene of wild enthusiasm we hoisted his big form upon our shoulders, and careered round the old quadrangle in triumph. Indeed he was the hero of our College life, leaving all others far behind, and impressing us with the idea that he had a boundless future before him."3

CHAPTER IV

THE STUDENT OF THEOLOGY

Over Cairns's life during his last session at the University there hung the shadow of a coming sorrow. His father's health, which had never been robust, and had been failing for some time, at length quite broke down; and it soon became apparent that, although he might linger for some time, there was no hope of his recovery. In the earlier days of his illness the father was able to write, and many letters passed between him and his student son. The following extracts from his letters reveal the character of the man, and surely furnish an illustration of what was said in a former chapter about the educative effect of religion on the Scottish working-man:—

"DUNGLASS, *Dec*, 23,1839.

"I would not have you think that I am overlooking the Divine agency in what has befallen me. I desire to ascribe all to His glory and praise, who can bring order out of confusion and light out of darkness; and I desire to look away from human means to Him who is able to kill and to make alive, knowing that He doth not grieve willingly nor afflict the children of men."

"DUNGLASS, *Jan.* 5, 1840.

"As I have no great pain except what arises from coughing, I have reason to bless the Lord, who is dealing so bountifully with me.... It would be unpardonable in me were I not endeavouring to make myself familiar with death in the forms and aspects in which he presents himself to the mind. Doubts and fears sometimes arise lest I should be indulging in a false and presumptuous hope, and, as there is great danger lest we should be deceived in this momentous concern, we cannot be too anxious in ascertaining whether our hope be that of the Gospel, as set forth in His Word of truth. Still, through the grace and mercy of the Lord Jesus Christ, whom, I trust upon scriptural grounds, I can call my Saviour, I am enabled to view death as a friend and as deprived of its sting, and this is a source of great comfort to me and cheers my drooping mind. I can say that my Beloved is mine and I am His, and that He will make all things to work together for His own glory and my eternal good. Dear son, I have thus opened my mind to you, and I trust that your prayers will not be wanting that my faith may be strengthened, and that all the graces of the Holy Spirit may abound in me, to the glory of God through our Lord Jesus Christ."

During this and part of the next year Cairns remained in Mr. Donaldson's family, and his relations with that family as a whole, as well as his special work in the tuition of the young son and daughter of the house, were of the most agreeable kind. He had by this time, however, formed some intimate friendships in Edinburgh, and there were several pleasant and interesting houses that were always open to him. One of these deserves special mention. Among his most intimate College friends was James McGibbon Russell, a distinguished student of Sir William Hamilton, and one of the founders of the Metaphysical Society. Russell was the son of a Perthshire parish minister, but his parents were dead, and he lived with an uncle and aunt, Mr. and Mrs. Archibald Wilson, whose own family consisted of two sons and three daughters. Cairns was introduced by Russell to the Wilson family, and soon became intimate with them. His special friend—at last the dearest friend he had in this world—was the younger son, George, afterwards the well-known chemist and Professor of Technology in the University of Edinburgh. No two men could be less alike—George Wilson with a bright, alert, nimble mind; Cairns with an intellect massive like his bodily frame, and characterised chiefly by strength and momentum; and yet the two fitted into each other, and when they really got to know each other it might truly be said of them that the love between them was wonderful, passing the love of women.

By the midsummer of 1840 Cairns had come to a final decision about his future calling. "I have," he wrote to his father on 13th June, "after much serious deliberation and prayer to God for direction, made up my mind to commence this year the study of divinity, with a view to the office of the ministry of the Gospel. I pray you, do implore the grace of God on my behalf, after this very grave and solemn determination."

The Secession Church, to which he belonged, and to whose ministry he desired to seek admission, had no theological tutors who were set apart for the work of teaching alone. Its professors, of whom there were four, were ministers in charges, who lectured to the students during the two holiday months of August and September. The curriculum of the "Divinity Hall," as it was called, consisted of five of these short sessions. During the remaining ten months of each year the student, except that he had to prepare a certain number of exercises for the Presbytery which had him under its charge, was left very much to do as he pleased.

Cairns entered the Hall, at that time meeting in Glasgow, in the August of 1840. Of the four professors who were on the staff of the institution, and all of whom were capable men, only two need here be mentioned. These were Dr. Robert Balmer of Berwick and Dr. John Brown of Edinburgh. Dr. Balmer was a clear-headed, fair-minded theologian—in fact, so very fair, and even generous, was he wont to be in dealing with opponents that he sometimes, quite unjustly, incurred the suspicion of being in sympathy, if not in league, with these opponents. He is specially interesting to us in this place, because Cairns succeeded him first in his pulpit, and then, after a long interval, in his chair. Dr. Brown, the grandson and namesake of the old commentator of Haddington, was a man of noble presence and noble character, whose personality "embedded in the translucent amber of his son's famous sketch" is familiarly known to all lovers of English literature. He was the pioneer of the scientific exposition of the Scriptures in the Scottish pulpit, and was one of the first exegetical theologians of his time. His point of view may be seen in a frequent criticism of his on a student's discourse: "That is truth and very important truth, but it is not *the* truth that is taught in this passage." Being so, it was simply "matter in the wrong place," *dirt* to be cleared away as speedily as possible.

Cairns had been first attracted to Dr. Brown by his speeches on the Annuity Tax, an Edinburgh ecclesiastical impost for which he had suffered the spoiling of his goods, and he had been for more than a year a member of his church in Broughton Place; but it was only now that he came to know him really well. Henceforth his admiration for Dr. Brown, and the friendship to which Dr. Brown admitted him, were to be amongst the most powerful influences of his life. Among his fellow-students at the Hall were several young men of brilliant promise, such as John Ker, who had been first prizeman in the Logic class in Hamilton's first session, W.B. Robertson, Alexander MacEwen, Joseph Leckie, and William Graham. Of these, Graham, bright, witty, versatile, the most notorious of punsters and the most illegible of writers, was his chief intimate, and their friendship continued unbroken and close for half a century.

But meanwhile the shadow was deepening over the home at Dunglass. All through the autumn and early winter his father was slowly sinking. He was only fifty-one, but he was already worn out; and his disease, if disease it might be called, had many of the symptoms of extreme old age. His son saw him for the last time near the close of the year. "I cannot say," he wrote to Miss Darling, "that depression of spirits was the only, or even the chief, emotion with which I bade farewell to my father. There was something so touching in his patience and resignation, so calm and inwrought in his meek submission to the Divine will, that it affected me more strongly than raptures of religious joy could have done. He displays the same evenness of temper in the sight of death as has marked his equable and consistent life."

He died in the early morning of 3rd January 1841. His son William thus describes the scene: "It was the first time any of us except our mother had looked on the face of the dying in the act of departing, and that leaves an impression that can never be effaced. When the end came, and each had truly realised what had happened, our mother in a broken voice asked that 'the Books' might be laid on the table; then she gave out that verse in the 107th Psalm—

'The storm is changed into a calm

At his command and will;

So that the waves that raged before,

Now quiet are and still.'

It was her voice, too, that raised the tune. Then she asked Thomas to read a chapter of the Bible and afterwards to pray. We all knelt down, and Thomas made a strong effort to steady his voice, but he failed utterly; then the dear mother herself lifted the voice of thanksgiving for the victory that had been won, and after that the neighbours were called in."[4]

Cairns was soon to have further experience of anxiety in respect to the health of those who were near to him. Towards the close of the year in which his father died, his brother William, who had almost completed his apprenticeship to a mason at Chirnside, in Berwickshire, was seized with inflammation, and for some weeks hung between life and death. At length he recovered sufficiently to be removed under his elder brother's careful and loving supervision to the Edinburgh Infirmary, where he remained for four months. During all that time Cairns visited his brother twice every day, he taught himself to apply to the patient the galvanic treatment which had been prescribed, and brought him an endless supply of books, periodicals, and good things to eat and smoke.

In the end of 1842 George Wilson was told by an eminent surgeon that he must choose between certain death and the amputation of a foot involving possible death. He agreed at once to the operation being performed, but begged for a week in which to prepare for it. He had always been a charming personality, and had lived a life that was outwardly blameless; but he had never given very serious thought to religion. Now, however, when he was face to face with death, the great eternal verities became more real to him, and during the week of respite the study of the New Testament and the counsel and sympathy and prayers of his friend Cairns prepared him to face his trial with calmness, and with "a trembling hope in Christ" in his heart. The two friends, who had thus been brought so closely together, were henceforth to be more to each other than they had ever been before.

The next year, 1843, was a memorable one in the ecclesiastical history of Scotland. Cairns, though not sympathising with the demand of the Non-Intrusion party in the Church of Scotland for absolute spiritual independence within an Established Church, had an intense admiration for

Chalmers, and was filled with the greatest enthusiasm when he and the party whom he led on the great 18th of May clung fast to the Independence and left the Establishment behind them. Indeed his enthusiasm ran positively wild, for it is recorded that, when the great procession came out of St. Andrew's Church, Cairns went hurrahing and tossing up his hat in front of it and all the way down the hill to Tanfield Hall. To Miss Darling, who had no sympathy with the Free Church movement, he wrote: "I know our difference of opinion here. But you will pardon me for saying that I have never felt more profound emotions of gratitude to God, of reverence for Christianity, of admiration of moral principle, and of pride in the honesty and courage of Scotsmen, than I did on that memorable day."

In the autumn of this year he was able to carry out a project which he had had before him, and for which he had been saving up his money for a long time. This was the spending of a year on the Continent. It was by no means so common in those days as it has since become for a Scottish theological student to attend a German University. Indeed, until the early Forties of last century, such a thing was scarcely known. Then, however, the influence of Sir William Hamilton, and the interest in German thought which his teaching stimulated, created the desire to learn more about it at its source.

It is natural that this movement should have affected the students of the Secession Church before it reached those of the Establishment; for not only were they less occupied with the great controversy of the day and its consequences, but their short autumn session left them free to take either a winter or a summer *semester*, or both, at a German University without interrupting their course at home. The late Dr. W.B. Robertson of Irvine used to lay claim to having been the pioneer of these "landlouping students of divinity." John Ker and others followed him; and when Cairns set out in 1843, quite a large company of old friends were expected to meet at Berlin. Cairns's departure was delayed by the illness of James Russell, who was to have accompanied him, but he set out towards the end of October. He had accepted an appointment as *locum tenens* for four weeks in an English Independent chapel at Hamburg, which delayed his arrival at Berlin until after the winter *semester* had commenced. But this interlude was greatly enjoyed both by himself and by the little company of English merchants who formed his first pastoral charge, and who, on a vacancy occurring, made a strong but fruitless attempt to induce him to remain as their permanent minister.

Arrived in Berlin, he joined his friends—Nelson, Graham, Wallace, and Logan Aikman. With Nelson he shared a room in the Luisenstrasse, where they set up that household god of all German students—a "coffee-machine," with the aid of which, and some flaming *spiritus*, they brewed their morning and evening beverage. They dined in the middle of the day at a neighbouring restaurant, on soup, meat, vegetables, and black bread, at a cost of threepence.

At the University, Cairns heard four or five lectures daily, taking among others the courses of Neander on Christian Dogmatics, Trendelenburg on History of Philosophy, and Schelling, the last of the great philosophers of the preceding generation, on Introduction to Philosophy. Of these, Schelling impressed him least, and Neander most. Through life he had a deep reverence for Neander, whom he regarded, with perhaps premature enthusiasm, as the man who shared with Schleiermacher the honour of restoring Germany to a believing theology.

Here is the description he gives of him in a letter from Berlin to George Wilson: "Suppose yourself in a large square room filled with Studiosi, each with his inkstand and immense *Heft* before him and ready to begin, when precisely at 11.15 a.m. in shuffles a little black Jew, without hat in hand or a scrap of paper, and strides up to a high desk, where he stands the whole time, resting his elbows upon it and never once opening his eyes or looking his class in the face; the worst type of Jewish physiognomy in point of intellect, though without its cunning or sensuality; the face meaningless, pale, and sallow, with low forehead, and nothing striking but a pair of enormous black eyebrows. The figure is dressed in a dirty brown surtout, blue plush trousers, and dirty top-boots. It begins to speak. The voice is loud and clear, and marches on with academic stateliness and gravity, and even something of musical softness mixes with its notes. Suddenly the speaker turns to a side. It is to spit, which act is repeated every second sentence. You now see in his hands a twisted pen, which is gradually stripped of every hair and then torn to pieces in the course of his mental working. His feet, too, begin to turn. The left pirouettes round and round, and at the close of an emphatic period strikes violently against the wall. When he has finished his lecture, you see only a mass of saliva and the rags of his pen. Neander is out of all sight the most wonderful being in the University. For knowledge, spirituality, good sense, and indomitable spirit of the finest discretion on moral subjects, the old man is a real marvel every way. In private he is the kindest but also the most awkward of mortals. His lectures on *Dogmatik* and *Sittenlehre* I value beyond all others, and I would gladly have come to Berlin to hear him alone."

Besides hearing these University lectures, Cairns read German philosophy and theology for nine or ten hours daily, took lessons in Hebrew from a young Christian Jew named Biesenthal,[5] and in these short winter months acquired such a mastery of German as a spoken language that in the spring he was urged by Professor Tholuck of Halle to remain and qualify as a Privatdocent at a German University. He also gained a knowledge of men and things German, and a living interest in them, which he retained through life.

At the close of the winter *semester*, the last weeks of which had been saddened by the news of James Russell's death; he set out on a tour extending over three months, and planned to include the principal cities and sights of Central and Southern Europe. He had only about £20 in his pocket, but he made this cover all the expenditure that was necessary for his modest wants. He travelled alone and, whenever it was possible, on foot, in the blouse and peaked cap of a German workman, and with a light knapsack strapped on his shoulders. He avoided hotels and lived cheaply, even meanly; but, with his splendid health, simple tastes, and overflowing interest in all that he saw, this did not greatly matter.

His classical studies, and an already wide knowledge of European history, suggested endless interesting associations with the places through which he passed; and the picture galleries furnished him with materials for art criticisms which, considering that he had had few opportunities of seeing paintings, surprise one by their insight and grasp. At Wittenberg we find him standing by the grave of Luther in the Castle Church, and reflecting on the connection between his presence there and the life and work of the man whose body lay below. "But for him there had neither been a Scotland to send out pilgrim students of theology, nor a Germany to receive them."

At Halle he has interesting interviews with Tholuck and Julius Müller; from Dresden he diverges to Herrnhut, where he witnesses the ordination of a Moravian missionary and takes part in a love-feast. At Prague, that wonderful city where the barbaric East begins, he finds his deepest interest stirred by the Jewish burying-ground and the hoary old synagogue. And so he passes on from city to city, and from land to land, by Vienna, Salzburg, and Munich, to Innsbruck, thence over the Brenner to Trent and Venice, and by Bologna to Florence and Rome. Returning by Genoa, Milan, and the Italian Lakes, he passes into Switzerland, and travels homeward by the Rhine. During this tour, when, in spite of the heat, he frequently walked forty-five or fifty miles a day, he had little time for letter-writing; but a small paper-covered book, in which he each night jotted down in pencil his impressions of what he had seen during the past day, has fortunately been preserved. From this three brief extracts may be made, and may serve as specimens of the whole, which is virtually reproduced entire in Dr. MacEwen's Biography. The first contains a description of the Jewish cemetery at Prague: "Through winding, filthy, pent-up, and over-peopled lanes, in the part of the old town next the river, heaped up with old clothes, trinket-ware, villainous-looking bread, and horrid sausages, one attains to an open space irregularly and rudely walled in and full of graves. The monuments date from the tenth century. No language can give an idea of its first impression. At one end one sees innumerable masses of grey weather-beaten stones in every grotesque angle of incidence and coincidence, but all rude and mean, covered with mystic Hebrew letters and half-buried amid long grass, nettles, and weeds. The place looks exactly as if originally a collection of dunghills or, perhaps, of excavated earth, left to its natural course after the corpses had been thrown in and the rude billets set over them. The economy of the race is visible in their measure for the dead, and contrasts wonderfully with the roominess and delicate adornment of German churchyards in general. The hoar antiquity of the place is increased by a wilderness of alders which grow up around the walls and amidst the stones, twisted, tangled, stunted, desolately old and yet renewing their youth, a true type of the scattered, bruised, and peeled, yet ineradicable Israel itself."

An incident at Novi, between Genoa and Milan, is thus described: "I had strolled into a vineyard behind the town, quite lonely and crowned with one cottage. On one of the secluded paths I found a little girl lying on the grass, with her face turned up to the sun and fast asleep. The breeze played beautifully with her hair, and her dress fluttered and rustled, but there she lay, and nothing but the heaving of her frame, which could hardly be distinguished from the agitation of the wind, proved that she was only asleep. I stood gazing for a long while, thinking of the Providence that watched alike over the child in its slumberings and the pilgrim in his wanderings; and as I saw her companions playing at no great distance, I left the spot without awakening the absent little one. As I was passing the cottage door, however, I was overtaken by the mother in evident agitation. She pointed along the path I had come by, as if she feared her child had wandered to the highway or been lost amid the wild brushwood that grew on that side of the vineyard. I soon made her understand that the *piccolina* was just behind her, and waited till she bounded away and returned with the crying thing in her arms, loading it with gentle reproaches and me with warm expressions of gratitude."

At Milan it must be admitted that he goes into raptures over the Cathedral, but one is glad to note that he reserves an ample tribute of enthusiasm for the old church of St. Ambrose: "In the cloister of St. Ambrose I saw the famous cypress doors which the saint closed against Theodosius, time-worn but solid; the brazen serpent, the fine pulpit with the bas-relief of the Agape, and the veritable Episcopal chair of marble, with solid back and sides, and lions embossed at the corners, in which he sat in the councils of his presbyters. It is almost the only relic I have done any honour to. I knelt down and kissed it, and forgot for the time that I was both Protestant and Presbyterian."

After a stormy and perilous voyage from Antwerp, he reached Newcastle in the first week of August, and started at once for Edinburgh to be present at the opening of the Divinity Hall. At the Dunglass lodge-gate his brother David, who was waiting for a letter which he had promised to throw down from the "Magnet" coach as he passed, caught a hurried glimpse of him, lean and brown as a berry after his exertions and his exposure to the Italian sun. On the following Saturday he put his pedestrian powers to the proof by walking from Edinburgh to Dunglass, when he covered the thirty-five and a half miles in seven hours and fifty minutes, having stopped only twice on the way—once in Haddington to buy a biscuit, and once at a wayside watering-trough to take a drink.

The Hall session of 1844 was Cairns's last, and the next step for him to take in ordinary course was to apply to a Presbytery for license as a probationer. He had, however, some hesitation in taking this step, mainly because he was not quite clear whether the real work of his life lay in the discharge of the ordinary duties of the ministry, or whether he might not render better service by devoting himself, as opportunity offered, more exclusively to theological and literary work in behalf of the Christian faith. His friend Clark, whom he consulted in the matter, strongly urged him to decide in favour of the latter alternative. His speculative and literary faculties, he urged, had already been tested with brilliant results; his powers as a preacher, on the other hand, were as yet an unknown quantity, and Clark thought it doubtful if they would be appreciated by an average congregation. The struggle was severe while it lasted, but it ended in Cairns deciding to go on to the ministry in the ordinary way. In November 1844 be applied to the Edinburgh Presbytery of the Secession Church for license, and he received it at their hands in the following February. He had not long to wait for a settlement. Dr. Balmer of Berwick, one of his divinity professors, had died while he was in Switzerland, and on his deathbed had advised his congregation to wait until Cairns had finished his course before electing a successor. Accordingly, it was arranged that he should preach in Golden Square Church, Berwick, a few weeks after he received license. The result was that a unanimous and enthusiastic call was addressed to him. He received another invitation from Mount Pleasant Church, Liverpool, of which his friend Graham was afterwards minister; but, after some hesitation, he decided in favour of Berwick.

Meanwhile changes had been taking place in the home circle at Dunglass. His brother William, whose illness has been already referred to, had now passed beyond all hope of recovering the use of his limbs. Having set himself resolutely to a course of study and mental improvement under his brother John's guidance, he was able to accept a kindly proposal made to him by Sir John Hall of Dunglass, that he should become the teacher of the little roadside school at Oldcambus, which John had attended as a child. On the marriage of his eldest brother in the summer of 1845 the widowed mother came to keep house for him, and henceforth the Oldcambus schoolhouse became the family headquarters. But that summer brought sorrow as well as change. Another brother, James, a young man of vigorous mental powers, and originally of stalwart physique, who had been working at his trade as a tailor in Glasgow, fell into bad health, which soon showed the symptoms of rapid consumption. He came home hoping to benefit by the change, but it became increasingly clear that he had only come home to die. He lingered till the autumn, and passed away at Oldcambus at the end of September. It was with this background of change and shadow that the ordination of John Cairns took place at Berwick on August 6, 1845.

CHAPTER V

GOLDEN SQUARE

Berwick is an English town on the Scottish side of the Tweed. As all that remained to England of the Scottish conquests of Edward I., it was until the Union of the Crowns the Calais of Scotland. It thus came to be treated as in a measure separate from England although belonging to it, and was for a long time separately mentioned in English Acts of Parliament, as it still is in English Royal Proclamations. This status of semi-independence which it so long enjoyed has helped to give it an individuality more strongly marked than that of most English towns.

In religious matters Berwick has more affinity to Scotland than to England. John Knox preached in the town for two years by appointment of the Privy Council of Edward VI., and in harmony with his influence its religious traditions were in succeeding generations strongly Puritan, and one of its vicars, Luke Ogle, was ejected for Nonconformity in 1662.

After the Revolution of 1688 this tendency found expression in the rise and growth of a vigorous Presbyterian Dissent; and in the early years of the eighteenth century there were two flourishing congregations in the town in communion with the Church of Scotland. But as these soon became infected with the Moderatism which prevailed over the Border, new congregations were formed in connection with the Scottish Secession and Relief bodies, and it was of one of these—Golden Square Secession Church—that John Cairns became the fourth minister in 1845.

Berwick is one of the very few English towns which still retain their ancient fortifications. The circuit of the walls, which were built in the reign of Elizabeth, with their bastions, "mounts," and gates, is still practically complete, and is preserved with care and pride. A few ruins of the earlier walls, which Edward I. erected, and which enclosed a much wider area than is covered by the modern town, still remain; also such vestiges of the once impregnable Castle as have not been removed to make way for the present railway-station. Beyond this, there is little about Berwick to tell of its hoary antiquity and its eventful history. But its red-roofed houses, rising steeply from the left bank of the Tweed, and looking across the tidal river to the villages of Tweedmouth and Spittal, have a picturesqueness of their own, whether they are seen when the lights and shadows of a summer day are playing upon them, or when they are swathed in the white folds of a North Sea *haar*.

The Berwick people are shrewd, capable, and kindly, and combine many of the good qualities of their Scotch and Northumbrian neighbours. Their dialect is in some respects akin to the Lowland Scotch, with which it has many words in common; and it has also as a prominent feature that rising intonation, passing sometimes almost into a wail, which one hears all along the eastern Border. But the great outstanding characteristic of Berwick speech is the *burr* a rough guttural pronunciation of the letter "i." With nothing but the scanty resources of our alphabet to fall back upon, it is quite impossible to represent this peculiarity phonetically, but it was once remarked by a student of Semitic tongues that the sound of the Hebrew letter 'Ayin is as nearly as possible that of the burr, and that, if you want to ascertain the correct Hebrew pronunciation of the name *Ba'al*, all you have got to do is to ask any Alderman of Berwick to say "*Barrel*"[6]

In 1845 the population of Berwick was between 8000 and 9000. "It included," says Dr. MacEwen, "some curious elements." Not the least curious and dubious of these was that of the lower class of the old Freemen of the Borough. These men had an inherited right to the use of lands belonging to the Corporation, which they let; and to a vote at a Parliamentary election, which they sold. When an election drew near, it was a maxim with both political parties that the Freemen must be conciliated at all costs; and the Freemen, knowing this, were quite prepared to presume on their knowledge. Once, at an election time, it happened that in the house of a prominent political leader in Berwick a fine roast of beef was turning before the kitchen fire, and was nearly ready for the dinner table, when a Freeman walked in, lifted it from the spit, and carried it off. No one dared to say him nay, for had he not a vote? and might not that vote turn the election?

At the other end of the social scale were the half-pay officers, the members of neighbouring county families, and the attorneys and doctors, who in some degree constituted the aristocracy of Berwick, and most of whom attended the Episcopalian Parish Church. The bulk of the shopkeepers and tradesmen, with some of the professional men and a large proportion of the working people, were Dissenters, and were connected with one or other of the half-dozen Presbyterian congregations in the town. Of these that of which Cairns was the minister was the most influential and the largest, having a membership of about six hundred.

The church was in Golden Square, of which it may be said that it is neither a square nor yet golden, but a dingy close or court opening by an archway from the High Street, the main thoroughfare of Berwick. The building was till recently a tannery, but the main features of it are still quite distinguishable. It stood on the left as one entered from High Street, and it had the usual high pulpit at its farther end, with a precentor's desk beneath it, and the usual deep gallery supported on metal pillars running round three of its four sides. The manse, its door adorned with a decent brass knocker, stood next to the church, on the side farthest from the street. It gave one a pleasant surprise on entering it to find that only its back windows looked out on the dim little "square." In front it commanded a fine view of the river, here crossed by a quaint old bridge of fifteen arches, which, owing to the exigencies of the current, is much higher at the Berwick end than at the other, and, as an Irishman once remarked, "has its middle all on one side." For some little time, however, after Cairns's settlement, he did not occupy the manse, but lived in rooms over a shop in Bridge Street; and when at length he did remove into it, he took his landlady with him and still remained her lodger.

For the first five years of his ministry Cairns devoted himself entirely to the work which it entailed upon him, and steadily refused to be drawn aside to the literary and philosophical tasks which many of his friends urged him to undertake. He had decided that his work in Berwick demanded his first attention, and, until he could ascertain how much of his time it would absorb, he felt that he could not go beyond it. On the early days of the week he read widely and hard on the lines of his Sunday work, and the last three days he devoted to writing out and committing to memory his two sermons, each of which occupied about fifty minutes in delivery. The "committing" of his sermons gave him little or no trouble, and he soon found that it could be relegated without anxiety to Saturday evening. And he got into the habit of preparing for it by a Saturday afternoon walk to the little yellow red-capped lighthouse at the end of Berwick Pier. At the upper end of the pier was a five-barred gate, and on the way back, when he thought that nobody was looking, he would vault over it with a running leap.

His preaching from the first made a deep impression. Following the old Seceder tradition, and the example of his boyhood's minister Mr. Inglis, and of his professor Dr. Brown, his discourse in the forenoon was always a "lecture" expository of some extended passage of Scripture, and forming one of a consecutive series; while that in the afternoon followed the familiar lines of an ordinary sermon. But there was nothing quite ordinary in his preaching at any time. Even when there was no unusual flight of eloquence, there was always to be noted the steady march of a strong mind from point to point till the conclusion had been reached; always a certain width and elevation of view, and always the ring of irresistible conviction. And although the discourse had been committed to memory and was reproduced in the very words that had been written down in the study, no barrier was thereby interposed between the preacher and his hearers. Somehow—at least after the first few paragraphs—when he had properly warmed to his work, the man himself seemed to break through all restraints and come into direct and living contact with his hearers.

His action sermon, *i.e.* the sermon preached before the Communion, was always specially memorable and impressive. He had the subject chosen weeks, and sometimes even months, beforehand, and, as he had no other sermon to write for the Communion Sunday, he devoted the whole of the preceding week to its preparation. His action sermons, which were those he usually preached on special occasions when he was away from home, dealt always with some theme connected with the Person or Work of Christ. They were frequently apologetic in their conception and structure, full of massive argument, which he had a remarkable power of marshalling and presenting so as to be understood by all; but the argument, reinforced by bursts of real eloquence, always converged on the, exaltation of the Redeemer. "I never thought so much of him as I do to-day," said one of his hearers to another after one of these sermons, "I never thought so much of Christ as I do to-day," replied the other; and that reply showed that in at least one case the purpose of the preacher in preparing and delivering his sermon had been fulfilled.

On the Sunday evening Cairns had a Bible-class of over one hundred young men and women, to which he devoted great care and attention. "It was the best hour of the day to us," wrote one who was a member of this class. "He was nearer us, and we were nearer him, than in church. The grandeur and momentum of his pulpit eloquence were not there, but we had instead a calm, rich, conversational instruction, a quiet disclosure of vast stores of information, as well as a definite dealing with young hearts and consciences, which left an unfading impression."

But Cairns was no mere preacher and teacher. He put out his full strength as truly in his pastoral work as in his work for and in the pulpit. He visited his large congregation statedly once a year, offering prayer in each house, and hearing the children repeat a psalm or portion of Scripture which he had prescribed the year before. He timed these visits so accurately that he could on one occasion banter one of his elders on the fact that he had received more than his due in one year, because the last visitation had been on the 1st of January and this one was on the 31st of December. A good part of his visiting had to be done in the country, because a considerable section of his congregation consisted of farmers or hinds from Northumberland, from the "Liberties of Berwick," and even from Scotland, which first begins three miles out from the town. These country visitations usually concluded with a service in a barn or farm-kitchen, to which worshippers came from far and near.

But besides this stated and formal visitation, which was intimated from the pulpit, constant attention was bestowed on the sick, the bereaved, the poor, the tempted, and all others who appealed specially to the minister's heart or his conscience. And yet there was no sense of task-work or of a burden to be borne about his relations to his congregation. His exuberant frankness of manner, contrasting as this did with the reserved and somewhat stiff bearing of his predecessor Dr. Balmer, won the hearts of all. And his keen sense of the ludicrous side of things often acted as an antiseptic, and kept him right both with himself and with his people.

Once, however, as he used to tell, it brought him perilously near to disaster. He was in the middle of his sermon one Sunday afternoon in Golden Square. It was a hot summer day, and all the doors and windows were open. From the pulpit he could look right out into the square, and as he looked he became aware of a hen surrounded by her young family pecking vigorously on the pavement in search of food, and clucking as she pecked. All at once an overwhelming sense of the difference between the two worlds in which he and that hen were living took possession of him, and it was with the utmost difficulty that he restrained himself from bursting into a shout of laughter. As it was, he recovered himself with a mighty gulp and finished the service decorously enough.

Cairns was also assisted in his work by his phenomenal powers of memory. After reading a long sermon once, or at most twice over, he could repeat it verbatim. Once when he was challenged by a friend to do so, he repeated, without stopping, the names of all the children in his congregation, apologising only for his imperfect acquaintance with two families who had recently come. Another instance of this is perhaps not so remarkable in itself, but it is worth mentioning on other grounds. Five-and-thirty years after the time with which we are now dealing, when he was a professor in Edinburgh, some of his students were carrying on mission work in a growing district of the city. An iron church was erected for them, but the contractor, an Englishman, before his work was finished was seized with illness and died. He was buried in one of the Edinburgh cemeteries, and Dr. Cairns attended the funeral. Having ascertained from the widow of the dead man that he had belonged to the Church of England, he repeated at the grave-side the whole of the Anglican Burial Service. When he was asked afterwards how he had thus come to know that Service without book, he replied that he had unconsciously got it by heart in the early days of his Berwick ministry, before there was either a cemetery or a Burials Act, when he had been compelled to stand silent and hear it read at the funerals of members of his own congregation in the parish churchyard.

Rather more than a year and a half after his ordination, in May 1847, the Secession Church in which he had been brought up, and of which he was now a minister, entered into a union with another of the Scottish non-Established Churches, the Synod of Relief. There was thus formed the United Presbyterian Church, with which his name was afterwards to be so closely associated. The United Church comprised five hundred and eighteen congregations, of which about fifty were, like those in Berwick, in England; the nucleus of that English Synod which, thirty years later, combined with the English Presbyterian Church to form the present Presbyterian Church of England. References in his correspondence show that this union of 1847, which afterwards had such happy results, excited at the time little enthusiasm, and was entered into largely as a matter of duty. "It is," he writes, "like the union, not of two globules of quicksilver which run together of themselves, but of two snowballs or cakes of mud that need in some way very tough outward pressure. I hope that the friction will elicit heat, since this neither cold nor hot spirit is not to edification."

The other letters of this period range over a wide variety of subjects. With John Clark he compares experiences of ministerial work; with John Nelson he discusses European politics as these have been affected by the events of the "year of revolutions," 1848; with George Wilson he discourses on every conceivable topic, from abstruse problems of philosophy and theology to the opening of the North British Railway; while his mother and his brothers, William and David, the latter of whom about this time left his work in the Dunglass woods to study for the ministry, are kept in touch with all that he knows they will best like to hear about. But in all this wide field of human life and thought and activity, which he so eagerly traverses, it is quite evident that what attracts him most is the relation of it all to a higher and an eternal order. With him the main interest is a religious one. Without an atom of affectation, and without anything that is at all morbid on his part, he reveals this at a hundred points. In this connection a letter which he wrote to Sir William Hamilton and which has since become well known, may be quoted here; and it, with Sir William's reply, will fittingly conclude the present chapter. This letter bears date November 16, 1848, and is as follows:—

"I herewith enclose the statement respecting the Calabar Mission of our Church, which I take blame to myself for having so long delayed to send. My avocations are very numerous, and a habit of procrastination, where anything is to be written, has sadly grown on me with time. I cannot even send you this brief note without testifying, what I could not so well utter in your presence, my unabated admiration of your philosophical genius and learning, and my profoundly grateful sense of the important benefits received by me both from your instructions and private friendship, I am more indebted to you for the foundation of my intellectual habits and tastes than to any other person, and shall bear, by the will of the Almighty, the impress of your hand through any future stage of existence. It is a relief to my own feelings to speak in this manner, and you will forgive one of the most favoured of your pupils if he seeks another kind of relief—a relief which he has long sought an opportunity to obtain—the expression of a wish that his honoured master were one with himself in the exercise of the convictions, and the enjoyment of the comforts, of living Christianity, or as far before himself as he is in all other particulars. This is a wish, a prayer, a fervent desire often expressed to the Almighty Former and Guide of the spirits of men, mingled with the hope that, if not already, at least some time, this accordance of faith will be attained, this living union realised with the great Teacher, Sacrifice, and Restorer of our fallen race. You will pardon this manifestation of the gratitude and affection of your pupil and friend, who, if he knew a higher, would gladly give it as a payment of a debt too great to be expressed. I have long ago been taught to feel the vanity of the world in all its forms—to renounce the hope of intellectual distinction, and to exalt love above knowledge. Philosophy has been to me much; but it can never be all, never the most; and I have found, and know that I have found, the true good in another quarter. This is mysticism—the mysticism of the Bible—the mysticism of conscious reconciliation and intimacy with the living Persons of the Godhead—a mysticism which is not like that of philosophy, an irregular and incommunicable intuition, but open to all, wise and unwise, who take the highway of humility and prayer. If I were not truly and profoundly happy in my faith—the faith of the universal Church—I would not speak of it. The greatest increase which it admits of is its sympathetic kindling in the hearts of others, not least of those who know by experience the pain of speculation, the truth that he who increaseth knowledge increaseth sorrow. I know you will indulge these expressions to one more in earnest than in former years, more philanthropic, more confident that he knows in whom he has believed, more impressed with the duty of bearing everywhere a testimony to the convictions which have given him a positive hold at once of truth and happiness.

"But I check myself in this unwonted strain, which only your long-continued and singular kindness could have emboldened me to attempt; and with the utterance of the most fervent wishes for your health, academical success, and inward light and peace, I remain your obliged friend and grateful pupil."

To which Sir W. Hamilton replied as follows:—

"EDINBURGH, *Dec.* 4, 1848.

"I feel deeply obliged to you for the kindness of your letter, and trust that I shall not prove wholly unworthy of the interest you take in me. There is indeed no one with whom I am acquainted whose sentiments on such matters I esteem more highly, for there is no one who, I am sure, is more earnest for the truth, and no one who pursues it with more independence and, at the same time, with greater confidence in the promised aid of God. May this promised aid be vouchsafed to me."[7]

CHAPTER VI

THE CENTRAL PROBLEM

It was confidently expected, not merely by Cairns's personal friends but by others in a much wider circle, that he would make a name for himself in the world of letters and speculative thought. It was not only the brilliance of his University career that led to this expectation, for, remarkable as that career had been, there have been many men since his time who, so far as mere prize taking is concerned, have equalled or surpassed him—men who never aroused and would not have justified any high-pitched hopes about their future. But Cairns, in addition to gaining academic distinctions, seems to have impressed his contemporaries in a quite exceptional degree with a sense of his power and promise. Professor Masson, writing of him as he was in his student days, thus describes him: "There was among us one whom we all respected in a singular degree. Tall, strong-boned, and granite-headed, he was the student whom Sir William Hamilton himself had signalised and honoured as already a sterling thinker, and the strength of whose logic, when you grappled with him in argument, seemed equalled only by the strength of his hand-grip when you met him or bade him good-bye, or by the manly integrity and nobleness of his character."8 And again, writing of him as he was at a later date, the same critic gives this estimate of his old fellow-student's mental calibre: "I can name one former student of Sir William Hamilton's, now a minister in what would be accounted in England one of the straitest sects of Scottish Puritanism, and who has consecrated to the duties of that calling a mind among the noblest I have known and the most learned in pure philosophy. Any man who on any subject of metaphysical speculation should contend with Dr. Cairns of Berwick-on-Tweed, would have reason to know, ere he had done with him, what strength for offence and defence there may yet be in a Puritan minister's hand-grip."9

That this is no mere isolated estimate of a partial friend it would not be difficult to prove. This was what his friends thought of him, and what they had taught others outside to think of him too. The time, however, had now come when it had to be put to the proof. During the first five years of his ministry at Berwick, as we have seen, Cairns devoted himself entirely to his work in Golden Square. He must learn to know accurately how much of his time that work would take up, before he could venture to spend any of it in other fields. But in 1850 he felt that he had mastered the situation, and accordingly he began to write for the Press. The ten years between 1850 and 1860 were years of considerable literary activity with him, and it may be said at once that their output sustained his reputation, and even added to it. There falls to be mentioned first a Memoir of his friend John Clark, who, after a brief and troubled ministerial career, had died of cholera in 1849. Cairns's Life of him, prefixed to a selection from his Essays and Sermons, fills only seventy-seven small pages, and it is in form to a large extent a defence of metaphysical studies against those who regard them as dangerous to the Christian student. But it contains many passages of great beauty and tenderness, and delineates in exquisite colours the poetry and romance of College friendships. "I am greatly charmed," wrote the author of *Rab and his Friends* to Cairns, "with your pages on the romance of your youthful fellowship—that sweet hour of prime. I can remember it, can feel it, can scent the morn."10

In 1850 the *North British Review*, which had been started some years previously in the interests of the Free Church, came under the editorship of Cairns's friend Campbell Fraser. Although he was a Free Church professor, he resolved to widen the basis of the *Review*, and he asked Cairns to join his staff, offering him as his province German philosophy and theology. Cairns assented, and promised to furnish two articles yearly. The first and most important of these was one which appeared in 1850 on Julius Müller's *Christian Doctrine of Sin*. This article, which is well and brightly written, embraces not merely a criticism of the great work whose name stands at the head of it, but also an elaborate yet most lucid and masterly survey of the various schools of theological thought which were then grouping themselves in Germany. Other contributions to the *North British* during the next four years included articles on "British and Continental Ethics and Christianity," on "The Reawakening of Christian Life in Germany," and on "The Life and Letters of Niebuhr"; while yet other articles saw the light in the *British Quarterly Review*, the *United Presbyterian Magazine*, and other periodicals. In 1858 appeared the important article on "Kant," in the eighth edition of the *Encyclopedia Britannica*, which was written at the urgent request of his friend Adam Black, and which cost him ten months reading and preparation.

As has been already said, his reputation appears to have been fully maintained by these articles. They brought him into touch with many interesting people, such as Bunsen and F.D. Maurice; and, in Scotland, deepened the impression that he was a man with a future. In 1852 John Wilson resigned the Professorship of Moral Philosophy in the University of Edinburgh, and the Town Council, who were the patrons of the chair, took occasion to let Cairns know that he might have the appointment if he desired it. He declined their offer, and with characteristic reticence said nothing about it either to his relatives or to his congregation. He threw himself, however, with great ardour into the support of the candidature of his friend Professor P.C. M'Dougall, who ultimately was elected to the post.

Four years later Sir William Hamilton died, and a fierce fight ensued as to who was to be his successor. The two most prominent candidates were Cairns's friend Campbell Fraser, then Professor of Logic in the New College, Edinburgh, and Professor James Frederick Ferrier of St. Andrews. Fraser was then a Hamiltonian and Ferrier was a Hegelian, and a great hubbub arose between the adherents of the two schools. This was increased and embittered by the importation of ecclesiastical and political feeling into the contest; Fraser being a Free Churchman, and Ferrier receiving the support of the Established Church and Tory party. The Town Council were very much at sea with regard to the philosophical controversy, and, through Dr. John Brown, they requested Cairns to explain its merits to them. Cairns responded by publishing a pamphlet entitled *An Examination of Professor Ferrier's Theory of Knowing and Being.* This pamphlet had for its object to show that Ferrier's election would mean a renunciation of the doctrines which, as expounded by Hamilton, had added so greatly to the prestige of the University in recent times as a school of philosophy, and also to expose what the writer conceived to be the dangerous character of Ferrier's teaching in relation to religious truth. It increased the storm tenfold. Replies were published and letters sent to the newspapers abusing Cairns, and insinuating that he had been led by a private grudge against Ferrier to take the step he had taken. It was also affirmed that he was acting at the instigation of the Free Church, who wanted to abolish their chair of Logic in the New College, but could not well do so so long as they had its present incumbent on their hands. A doggerel parody on *John Gilpin,* entitled "The Diverting History of John Cairns," in which a highly coloured account is given of the supposed genesis of the pamphlet, was written and found wide circulation. The first two stanzas of this effusion were the following:—

"John Cairns was a clergyman

  Of credit and renown,

A first-rate U.P. Church had he

  In far-famed Berwick town.

John likewise had a loving friend,

  A mighty man of knowledge,

The Rev. A.C. Fraser, he

  Of the sanctified New College."

Cairns found it needful to issue a second pamphlet, *Scottish Philosophy: a Vindication and Reply*, in which, while tenaciously holding to what he had said in the last one, he challenged Ferrier to mention one single instance in which he had made a personal attack on him. When at length the vote came to be taken, and Fraser was elected by a majority of three, there were few who doubted that the intervention of the Berwick minister had been of critical importance in bringing about this result.

Two years later George Wilson, who was now a professor in the University, had the satisfaction of intimating to his friend that his *alma mater* had conferred on him the degree of D.D., and in the following year (1859) a much higher honour was placed within his reach. The Principalship of the University became vacant by the death of Dr. John Lee, and the appointment to the coveted post, like that to the two professorships, was in the hands of the Town Council. It was informally offered to Cairns through one of the councillors, but again he sent a declinature, and again he kept the matter carefully concealed. It was not, in fact, until after his death, when the correspondence regarding it came to light, that even his own brothers knew that at the age of forty this great and dignified office might have been his.

These declinatures on Cairns's part of philosophical posts, or posts the occupation of which would give him time and opportunity for doing original work in philosophy, are not on the whole difficult to understand when we bear in mind his point of view. He had, after careful deliberation, given himself to the Christian ministry, and he meant to devote the whole of his life to its work. He was not to be turned aside from it by the attractions of any employment however congenial, or of any leisure however splendid. His speculative powers had been consecrated to this object, as well as his active powers, and would find their natural outlet in harmony with it. And so the hopes of his friends and his own aspirations must be realised in his work, not in the field of philosophy but in that of theology. Accordingly, he decided to follow up his work in the periodicals by writing a book. He took for his subject "The Difficulties of Christianity," and made some progress with it, getting on so far as to write several chapters. Then he was interrupted and the work was laid aside. The great book was never written, nor did he ever write a book worthy of his powers. A moderate-sized volume of lectures on "Unbelief in the Eighteenth Century," a volume of sermons, most of which were written in the first fifteen years of his ministry, a Memoir of Dr. Brown,—these, with the exception of a quantity of pamphlets, prefaces, and magazine articles, were all that he gave to the world after the time with which we are now dealing. How are we to account for this? The time in which he lived was a time of great intellectual activity and unsettlement—time that, in the opinion of most, needed, and would have welcomed, the guidance he could have given;

and yet he stayed his hand. Why did he do so? This is the central problem which a study of his life presents, and it is one of no ordinary complexity; but there are some considerations relating to it which go far to solve it, and these it may be worth while for us at this point to examine.

At the outset, something must be allowed for the special character of the influence exerted on Cairns by Sir William Hamilton. That influence was profound and far-reaching. In the letter to Hamilton which was quoted at the end of the preceding chapter, Cairns tells his master that he must "bear, by the will of the Almighty, the impress of his hand through any further stage of existence," and, strong as the expression is, it can scarcely be said to be an exaggeration. But Hamilton's influence, while it called out and stimulated his pupil's powers to a remarkable degree, was not one which made for literary productiveness. He was a great upholder of the doctrine that truth is to be sought for its own sake and without reference to any ulterior end, and he had strong ideas about the discredit—the shamefulness, as it seemed to him—of speaking or writing on any subject until it had been mastered down to its last detail. This attitude prevented Hamilton himself from doing full justice to his powers and learning, and its influence could be seen in Cairns also—in his delight in studies the relevancy of which was not always apparent, and in a certain fastidiousness which often delayed, and sometimes even prevented, his putting pen to paper.

But another and a much more important factor in the problem is to be found in the old Seceder ideal of the ministry in which he was trained and which he never lost. It has been truly said of him that "he never all his life got away from David Inglis and Stockbridge any more than Carlyle got away from John Johnston and Ecclefechan." According to the Seceder view, there is no more sublime calling on earth than that of the Christian ministry, and that calling is one which concerns itself first and chiefly with the conversion of sinners and the edifying of saints. This work is so awful in its importance, and so beneficent in its results, that it must take the chief place in a minister's thoughts and in the disposition of his time; and if it requires the sole place, that too must be accorded to it. "To me," wrote Cairns to George Gilfillan in 1849, "love seems infinitely higher than knowledge and the noblest distinction of humanity—the humble minister who wears himself out in labours of Christian love in an obscure retreat as a more exalted person than the mere literary champion of Christianity, or the recondite professor who is great at Fathers and Schoolmen. I really cannot share those longings for intellectual giants to confront the Goliath of scepticism—not that I do not think such persons useful in their way, but because I think Christianity far more impressive as a life than as a speculation, and the West Port evangelism of Dr. Chalmers far more effective than his Astronomical Discourses."11

It was to the ministry, as thus understood, that Cairns had devoted himself at the close of his University course and again just before he took license as a probationer, when for a short time, as we have seen, he had been drawn aside by the attractions of "sacred literature." He never thought of becoming a minister and was putting his main strength into philosophy and theology. Not that he now forswore all interest in either, but from the moment of his final decision, he had determined that the mid-current of his life should run in a different direction.

Yet another important factor in the case is to be found in the circumstances of his Berwick ministry. Had his lot been cast in a quiet country place, with only a handful of people to look after, the great book might yet have been written. But he had to attend to a congregation whose membership was at first nearly six hundred, and afterwards rose to seven hundred and eighty and, with his standard of pastoral efficiency, this left him little leisure. Indeed it is wonderful that, under these conditions, he accomplished so much as he did—that he wrote his *North British* articles, maintained a reputation which won for him so many offers of academic posts, and at the same time laid the foundation of a vast and spacious learning in Patristic and Reformation theology. Akin to his strictly ministerial work, and flowing out of it, was the work he did for his Church as a whole—the share he took in the Union negotiations with the Free Church during the ten years that these negotiations lasted, and the endless round of church openings and platform work to which his growing fame as a preacher and public speaker laid him open.

But there is one other consideration which, although it is to some extent involved in what has already been said, deserves separate and very special attention. Although his friends and the public regretted his withdrawal from the speculative field, it is not so clear that he regretted it himself. He had, it is true, worked in it strenuously and with conspicuous success, and had revealed a natural aptitude for Christian apologetics of a very high order. But it does not appear that either his heart or his conscience were ever fully engaged in the work. He never seemed as if he were fighting for his life, because he always seemed to have another and an independent ground of certainty on which he based his real defence. There is a passage in his Life of Clark which bears upon this point so closely that it will be well to quote it here:—

"The Christian student is as conscious of direct intercourse with Jesus Christ as with the external world, or with other minds. This is the very postulate of living Christianity. It is a datum or revelation made to a spiritual faculty in the soul, as real as the external senses or any of the mental or moral faculties, and far more exalted. This living contact with a living person by faith and prayer is, like all other life, ultimate and mysterious, and must be accepted by him in whom it exists as its own sufficient explanation and reason, just as the principles of natural intelligence and conscience, to which it is something superadded, and with which, in this point of view, though in other respects higher, it is co-ordinate. No one who is living in communion with Jesus Christ, and exercising that series of affections towards Him which Christianity at once prescribes and creates, can doubt the reality of that supernatural system to which he has been thus introduced; and nothing more is necessary than to appeal to his own experience and belief, which is here as valid and irresistible as in regard to the existence of God, of moral distinctions, or of the material world. He has no reason to trust the one class of beliefs which he has not, to trust the other.... To minds thus favoured, this forms a *point d'appui* which can never be overturned—an *aliquid inconcussum* corresponding to the '*cogito ergo sum*' of Descartes. Their faith bears its own signature, and they have only to look within to discover its authenticity. Philosophy must be guided by experience, and must rank the characters inscribed on the soul by grace at least as sacred as those inscribed by nature. Such persons need not that any man should teach them, for they have an unction from the Holy One; and to them applies the highest of all congratulations: 'Blessed art thou; for flesh and blood hath not revealed it unto thee, but My Father which is in heaven.'"12

These words contain the true explanation of Cairns's life. There was in it the "*aliquid inconcussum*"—the "unshaken somewhat"—which made him independent of other arguments, and which kept him untouched by all the intellectual attacks on Christianity. Other people who had not this inward testimony, or who, having it, could not regard it as unshaken by the assaults of infidelity, he could argue with and seek to meet them on their own intellectual ground; but for himself, any victories gained here were superfluous, any defects left him unmoved. Was it always so with him? Or was there ever a time when he was carried off his feet and had to struggle for dear life for his Christian faith amid the dark waters of doubt?

There are indications that on at least one occasion he subjected his beliefs to a careful scrutiny, and, referring to this later, he spoke of himself as one who, in the words of the Roman poet, had been "much tossed about on land and on the deep ere he could build a city." This, coming from one who was habitually reticent about his religious experiences, may be held as proving that there was no want of rigour in the process, no withholding of any part of the structure from the strain. But that that structure ever gave way, that it ever came tumbling down in ruins about him so that it had to be built again on new foundations, there is no evidence to show. The "*aliquid inconcussum*" appears to have remained with him all through the experience. This seems clear from a passage in a letter written in 1848 to his brother David, then a student in Sir William Hamilton's class, in which he says; "I never found my religious susceptibilities injured by metaphysical speculations. Whether this was a singular felicity I do not know, but I have heard others complain."13

This, taken in conjunction with the passage quoted above from Clark's Life, in which it is hard to believe that he is not speaking of himself, seems decisive enough, and in a mind of such speculative grasp and activity it is remarkable. "Right down through the storm-zone of the nineteenth century," writes one who knew him well, "he comes untroubled by the force of the 'aliquid inconcussum.' Edinburgh, Germany, Berwick; Hamilton, Kant, Hegel, Strauss, Renan, it is all the same. The cause seems to me luminously plain. Saints are never doubters. His religious intuitions were so deep and clear that he was able always to find his way by their aid. They gave him his independent certainty, his 'aliquid inconcussum.'"

His influence on the religious life of his time was largely due to the spiritual faculty in him that is here referred to. He was the power he was, not so much because of his intellectual strength as because of his character,—because he was "a great Christian." But in this respect he had the defects of his qualities; and it is open to question whether he ever truly appreciated the formidable character of modern doubt, just because he himself had never had full experience of its power, because the iron of it had never really entered into his soul.

George Gilfillan, who, with all his defects, had often gleams of real insight, wrote thus in his diary 14th January 1863: "I got yesterday sent me, per post, a lecture by John Cairns on 'Rationalism, Ritualism, and Pure Religion,' or some such title, and have read it with interest, attention, and a good deal of admiration of its ability and, on the whole, of its spirit. But I can see from it that he is not the man to grapple with the scepticism of the age. He has not sufficient sympathy with it, he has not lived in its atmosphere, he has not visited its profoundest or tossed in its stormiest depths. Intellectually and logically he understands it as he understands most other matters, but sympathetically and experimentally he does not."

There is a considerable amount of truth in this, although it is lacking somewhat in the sympathy which the critic desiderates in the man he is criticising. Cairns did not feel that the battle with modern doubt was of absolutely overwhelming importance, and this, along with the other things to which reference has been made, kept him from giving to the world that new statement of the Christian position which his friends hoped to get from him, and which he at one time hoped to be able to give.

CHAPTER VII

THE APOSTLE OF UNION

The close of the period dealt with in the last chapter was made sadly memorable to Cairns by the death of some of his closest friends. In October 1858 died the venerable Dr. Brown, with whom, since he was a student, he had stood in the closest relations, and whom he revered and habitually addressed as a father. In November 1859 the bright spirit of George Wilson, the dearest of all his friends, passed away; and in the same year he had to mourn the loss of Miss Darling, the correspondent and adviser of his student days. His brave old mother died in the autumn of 1860, and in the following year he lost another old and dear friend in Mrs. Balmer, the widow of his predecessor in Golden Square, who perhaps knew him better than his own mother, and had been deeper in his confidence than anyone since he came to Berwick. From this period he became more reserved. With all his frankness there was always a characteristic reticence about him, and this was less frequently broken now that those to whom he had so freely poured out his soul had been taken from him. But he drew closer to those who were still left—especially to his own kindred, to his sisters, to his brother William at Oldcambus, and to his brother David, who had now been settled for some years as minister at Stitchel, near Kelso.14

Dr. Brown had nominated him as one of his literary executors, and his family were urgent in their request that he should write their father's Life. With great reluctance he consented, and for eighteen months this task absorbed the whole of his leisure, to the complete exclusion of the work on "The Difficulties of Christianity," with which he had already made some progress. The undertaking was a labour of love, but it cannot be said to have been congenial. Memoir writing was not to his taste, and in this case he had made a stipulation that still further hampered him and made success very difficult. This was that he should omit, as far as possible, all personal details, and leave these to be dealt with in a separate chapter which Dr. Brown's son John undertook to furnish. This chapter was not forthcoming when the volume had to go to press, and was separately issued some months later. When the inspiration did at length come to "Dr. John," it came in such a way as to add a new masterpiece to English literature, and one which, while it gave a wonderfully living picture of the writer's father, disclosed to the world as nothing else has ever done the true *ethos* and inner life of the Scottish Secession Church. The Memoir itself, of which this "Letter to John Cairns, D.D." is the supplementary chapter, is a sound and solid bit of work, giving an accurate and interesting account of the public life of Dr. Brown and of the movements in which he took part. It is, as William Graham said of it, "a thoughtful, calm, conclusive book, perhaps too reticent and colourless, but none the less like Dr. Brown because of that."

No sooner was this book off his hands than Cairns was urged to undertake another biographical work—the Life of George Wilson. But this, in view of his recent experience, he steadfastly refused to do, and contented himself with writing a sketch of his friend for the pages of *Macmillan's Magazine*. When, however, Wilson's biography was taken in hand by his sister, Cairns promised to help her in every possible way with his advice and guidance, and this he did from week to week till the book was published. This help on his part was continued by his seeing through the press Wilson's posthumous book, *Counsels of an Invalid*, which appeared in 1862. With the completion of this task he seemed to be free to return to his theological work, and he did return to it; but his release turned out to be only a brief respite. In 1863 the ten years' negotiations for Union between the Free and United Presbyterian Churches, in which he felt impelled to take a prominent and laborious part, were begun, and they absorbed nearly all of his leisure during what might have been a productive period of his life. When he emerged from them he was fifty-four years of age, he had passed beyond the time of life when his creative powers were at their freshest, and the general habits of his life and lines of his activity had become settled and stereotyped.

This is not the place in which to enter into a detailed account of the Union negotiations. That has been done with admirable lucidity and skill by such writers as Dr. Norman Walker in his Life of Dr. Robert Buchanan, and by Dr. MacEwen in his Life of the subject of the present sketch, and it does not need to be done over again. But something must be said at this point to indicate the general lines which the negotiations followed and to make Cairns's relation to them clear. That he should have taken a keen and sympathetic interest in any great movement for ecclesiastical union was quite what might have been expected. What interested him in Christian truth, and what he had, ever since he had been a student, set himself specially to expound and defend, were the great catholic doctrines which are the heritage of the one Church of Christ. Constitutionally, he was disposed to make more of the things that unite Christians than of those which divide them; and, while he was loyally attached to his own Church, many of his favourite heroes, as well as many of his warmest personal friends, belonged to other Churches. Hence anything that made for Union was entirely in line with his feelings and his convictions. Thus he had thrown himself heartily into the work of the Evangelical Alliance, and at its memorable Berlin Meeting of 1857 had created a deep impression by an address which he delivered in German on the probable results of a closer co-operation between German and British Protestantism. In the same year he took part in a Conference in Edinburgh which had been summoned by Sir George Sinclair of Ulbster to discuss the possibility of Church Union at home. And when in 1859 the Union took place in the Australian Colonies of the Presbyterian Churches which bore the names of the Scottish Churches from which they had sprung, it was to a large extent through his influence that the Australian United Presbyterians took part in the Union.

His ideal at first was of one great Presbyterian Communion co-extensive with the English language, and separately organised in the different countries and dependencies in which its adherents were to be found, but having one creed and one form of worship and complete freedom from all State patronage and control. But, as the times did not seem ripe for such a vast consummation, he made no attempt to give his ideal a practical form, and concentrated his energies on the lesser movement which was beginning to take shape for a union of the Presbyterian Churches in England and the non-Established Presbyterian Churches in Scotland. He was one of those who brought this project before the Synod of the United Presbyterian Church in May 1863, when he appeared in support of an overture from the Berwick Presbytery in favour of Union. The overture was adopted with enthusiasm, and the Synod agreed by a majority of more than ten to one to appoint a committee to confer with a view to Union with any committee which might be appointed by the Free Church General Assembly. The Free Church Assembly, which met a fortnight later, passed a similar resolution unanimously, although not without a keen discussion revealing elements of opposition which were afterwards to gather strength.

It is quite possible that, as competent observers have suggested, if the enthusiasm for the project which then existed had been taken advantage of at once, Union might have been carried with a rush. But the able men who were guiding the proceedings thought it safer to advance more slowly; and, when the Joint Union Committee met, they went on to consider in detail the various points on which the two Churches differed. These had reference almost entirely to the relations between Church and State. The United Presbyterians were, almost to a man, "Voluntaries," *i.e.* they held that the Church ought in all cases to support itself without assistance from the State, and free from the interference which, in their view, was the inevitable and justifiable accompaniment of all State establishments. The Free Churchmen, on the other hand, while maintaining as their cardinal principle that the Church must be free from all State interference, and while therefore protesting against the existing Establishment, held that the Church, if its freedom were adequately guaranteed, might lawfully accept establishment and endowment from the State. An elaborate statement was drawn up exhibiting first the points on which the two Churches were agreed with regard to this question, and then the points on which they differed. From this it appeared that they were at one as to the duty of the State—or, in the language of the Westminster Confession, the "Civil Magistrate"—to make Christian laws and to administer them in a Christian spirit. The Civil Magistrate ought, it was agreed, to be a Christian, not merely as a man but as a magistrate. The only vital point of difference was with regard to the question of Church establishments—as to whether it was part of the Christian Civil Magistrate's duty to establish and endow the Church. But, as it seemed to be a vain hope that the Free Church would ever get an Establishment to its mind, it was urged that this was a mere matter of theory, and might be safely left as an "open question" in a United Church. The statement referred to, which is better known as the "Articles of Agreement," was not ready to be submitted in a final form to the Synod and Assembly of 1864, and the Committee, which was now reinforced by representatives from the Reformed Presbyterian Church and from the Presbyterian Church in England, was reappointed to carry on its labours.

But meanwhile clouds were beginning to appear on the horizon. In the United Presbyterian Synod there was a small minority of sturdy Voluntaries who, while not opposed to Union, were apprehensive that the price to be paid for it would be the partial surrender of their testimony in behalf of their distinctive principle. They did not wish to impose their beliefs on others, but they were anxious to reserve to themselves full liberty to hold and propagate their views in the United Church, and they were not sure that, by accepting the Articles of Agreement, they were in fact doing this. The efforts of Dr. Cairns and others were directed, not without success, to meeting their difficulties. But in the Free Church a more formidable opposition began to show itself. There had always been a conservative element in that Church, represented by men who held tenaciously to the more literal interpretation of its ecclesiastical documents and traditions; and, as the discussions went on, it became clear that the hopelessness of a reconciliation with the Establishment was not so universally felt as had been at first supposed. The supporters of the Union movement included almost all the trusted leaders of the Church—men like Drs. Candlish, Buchanan, Duff, Fairbairn, Rainy, and Guthrie, Sir Henry Moncreiff, Lord Dalhousie, and Mr. Murray Dunlop, most of whom had got their ecclesiastical training in the great controversy which had issued in the Disruption; but all their eloquence and all their skill did not avail to allay the misgivings or silence the objections of the other party. At length in 1867 a crisis was reached. The Articles of Agreement, after having been finally formulated by the Committee, had been sent down to Presbyteries for their consideration; and the reports of the Presbyteries were laid on the table of the Assembly of that year. The question now arose, Was it wise, in view of the opposition, to take further steps towards Union? The Assembly by 346 votes to 120 decided to goon; whereupon the Anti-Union leaders resigned the seats which up to this time they had retained on the Union Committee.

It is true that, after the Committee had been relieved of this hostile element, considerable and rapid progress was made. Hopes were cherished for a time that the Union might yet be consummated, and the determination was expressed to carry it through at all hazards. But the Free Church minority, ably led and knowing its own mind, stubbornly maintained its ground. Its adherents, who included perhaps one-third of the ministers and people of the Church, were specially numerous in the Highlands, where United Presbyterianism was practically unrepresented.

Here most distorted views were held of the Voluntaryism which most of its ministers and members professed. It was represented as equivalent to National Atheism, and from this the transition was an easy one, especially in districts where few of the people had even seen a United Presbyterian, to the position that an upholder of National Atheism must himself be an Atheist. It became increasingly clear, as the years passed, that if the Union were to be forced through, there must be a new Disruption, and a Disruption which would cost the Free Church those Highland congregations which for thirty years it had been its glory to maintain. Moreover, it was currently reported that the Anti-Union party had taken the opinion of eminent counsel, and that these had declared that, in the event of a Disruption taking place on this question of Union, the protesting minority would be legally entitled to take with them the entire property of the Church. The conviction was forced on the Free Church leaders (and in this they were supported by their United Presbyterian brethren) that the time was not yet ripe for that which they so greatly desired to see, and that even for Union the price they would have to pay was too great. And so with heavy hearts they decided in 1873 to abandon the negotiations which had been proceeding for ten years. All that they felt themselves prepared to carry was a proposal that Free Church or United Presbyterian ministers should be "mutually eligible" for calls in the two Churches—a proposal that did not come to much.

Three years later, the Reformed Presbyterian Church united with the Free Church, and in the same year (1876) the United Presbyterian Church gave up one hundred and ten of its congregations, which united with the English Presbyterian Church and thus formed the present Presbyterian Church of England. The original idea, at least on the United Presbyterian side, had been that all the negotiating bodies should be welded into one comprehensive British Church; but this, especially in view of the breakdown of the larger Union, proved to be unworkable, and the final result for the United Presbyterians was that they came out of the negotiations a considerably smaller and weaker Church than they had been when they went into them.

In all the labours and anxieties of these ten years Dr. Cairns had borne a foremost part. At the meetings of the Union Committee he took an eager interest and a leading share in the discussions; and, while never compromising the position of his Church, he did much to set it in a clear and attractive light. In the United Presbyterian Synod, where it fell to his lot year by year to deliver the leading speech in support of the Committee's report, his eloquence, his sincerity, and his enthusiasm did not a little to reassure those who feared that there was a tendency on the part of their representatives to concede too much, and did a very great deal to keep his Church as a whole steadily in favour of Union in spite of many temptations to have done with it. Dr. Hutton, one of those advanced Voluntaries who had never been enthusiastic about the Union proposals, wrote to him at the close of the negotiations: "We have reached this stage through your vast personal influence more than through any other cause."

Outside of the Church Courts he delivered innumerable speeches at public meetings which had been organised in all parts of the country in aid of the Union cause. These more than anything else led him to be identified in the public mind with that cause, and gained for him the name of the "Apostle of Union." The meetings at which these speeches were delivered were mostly got up on the Free Church side, where there seemed to be more need of missionary work of this kind than on his own, and his appearances on these occasions increased the favour with which he was already regarded in Free Church circles. "The chief attraction of Union for me," an eminent Free Church layman is reported to have said, "is that it will bring me into the same Church with John Cairns."

That he was deeply disappointed by the failure of the enterprise on which his hopes had been so much set, he did not conceal; but he never believed that the ten years' work had been lost, and he never doubted that Union would come. He did not live to see it, but when, on October 31, 1900, the two Churches at length became one, there were many in the great gathering in the Waverley Market who thought of him, and of his strenuous and noble labours into which they were on that day entering. Dr. Maclaren of Manchester gave expression to these thoughts in his speech in the evening of the day of Union, when, after paying a worthy tribute to the great leader to whose skill and patience the goodly consummation was so largely due, he went on to say: "But all during the proceedings of this day there has been one figure and one name in my memory, and I have been saying to myself, What would John Cairns, with his big heart and his sweet and simple nature, have said if God had given him to see this day! 'These all died in faith, not having received the promises... God having provided some better thing for us.'"

CHAPTER VIII

WALLACE GREEN

All the time occupied by the events described in the last two chapters, Dr. Cairns was carrying on his ministry in Berwick with unflagging diligence. True to his principle, he steadily devoted to his pulpit and pastoral work the best of his strength, and always let them have the chief place in his thoughts. He gave to other things what he could spare, but he never forgot that he had determined to be a minister first of all. His congregation had prospered greatly under his care, and in 1859 the old-fashioned meeting-house in Golden Square was abandoned for a stately and spacious Gothic church with a handsome spire which had been erected in Wallace Green, with a frontage to the principal open square of the town. A few years earlier a new manse had been secured for the minister. This manse is the end house of a row of three called Wellington Terrace. These stand just within the old town walls, which are here pierced by wide embrasures. They are separated from the walls by a broad walk and a row of grass-plots, alternating with paved spaces opposite the embrasures, on which cannon were once planted. The manse faces south, and is roomy and commodious. When Dr. Cairns moved into it, he had an elderly servant as his housekeeper, of whom he is said to have been not a little afraid; but, after a couple of years or so, his sister Janet was installed as mistress of his house; and during the remaining thirty-six years of his life she attended to his wants, looked after his health, and in a hundred prudent and quiet ways helped him in his work.

The study at Wellington Terrace is upstairs, and is a large room lighted by two windows. One of these looks across the river, which at this point washes the base of the town walls, to the dingy village of Tweedmouth, rising towards the sidings and sheds of a busy railway-station and the Northumberland uplands beyond. The other looks right out to sea, and when it is open, and sometimes when it is shut, "the rush and thunder of the surge" on Berwick bar or Spittal sands can be distinctly heard. In front, the Tweed pours its waters into the North Sea under the lee of the long pier, which acts as a breakwater and shelters the entrance to the harbour. Far away to the right, Holy Island, with the castle-crowned rock of Bamborough beyond it, are prominent objects; and at night, the Longstone light on the Outer Farne recalls the heroic rescue by Grace Darling of the shipwrecked crew of the *Forfarshire*.

Opposite this window stood the large bookcase in which Dr. Cairns's library was housed. The books composing the library were neither very numerous, very select, nor in very good condition. Although he was a voracious reader, it must be admitted that Dr. Cairns took little pride in his books. It was a matter of utter indifference to him whether he read a favourite author in a good edition or in a cheap one. The volumes of German philosophy and theology, of which he had a fair stock, remained unbound in their original sober livery, and when any of them threatened to fall to pieces he was content to tie them together with string or to get his sister to fasten them with paste. One or two treasures he had, such as a first edition of Bacon's *Instauratio Magna*, a first edition of Butler's *Analogy*, and a Stephens Greek Testament; also a complete set of the Delphin Classics, handsomely bound, and some College prizes. These, with the Benedictine edition of Augustine, folio editions of Athanasius, Chrysostom, and other Fathers, some odd volumes of Migne, and a considerable number of books on Reformation and Secession theology, formed the most noteworthy elements in his collection. He added later a very complete set of the writings of the English Deists, and the works of Voltaire, Rousseau, and Renan. Side by side with these was what came to be a vast accumulation of rubbish, consisting of presentation copies of books on all subjects which his anxious conscience persuaded him that he was bound to keep on his shelves, since publishers and authors had been kind enough to send them to him. Nearly all the books that belonged to his real library he had read with care. Most of them were copiously annotated, and his annotations were, as a rule, characterised by a refreshing trenchancy,—in the case of some, as of Gibbon, tempered with respect; in the case of others, as of F.W. Newman and W.R. Greg, bordering on truculence. The only other noteworthy objects in the study were two splendid engravings of Raphael's "Transfiguration" and "Spasimo" (the former bearing the signature of Raphael Morghen), which had been a gift to him from Mrs. Balmer.

The greater part of each day was spent in this room. He could get along with less sleep than most men; and however late he might have sat over his books at night, he was frequently in his study again long before breakfast. After breakfast came family worship, each item of which was noteworthy. Although passionately fond of sacred music, he had a wild, uncontrollable kind of voice in singing. He seemed to have always a perfectly definite conception of what the tune ought to be, but he was seldom able to give this idea an accurate, much less a melodious, expression. Yet he never omitted the customary portion of psalm or hymn, but tackled it with the utmost gallantry, fervour, and enthusiasm, although he scarcely ever got through a verse without going off the tune.

His reading of Scripture had no elocutionary pretensions about it; it was quiet, and to a large extent gone through in a monotone; but two things about it made it very impressive. One of these was the deep reverence that characterised it, and the other was a note of subdued enthusiasm that ran all through it. It was clear to the listener that behind every passage read, whether it was history, psalm, or prophecy, or even the driest detail of ritual, there was visible to him a great world-process going on that appealed to his imagination and influenced even the tones of his voice. And his prayers, quite unstudied as they of course were, brought the whole company right into the presence of the Unseen. They were usually full of detail,—he seemed to remember everybody and everything,—but each petition was absolutely appropriate to the special case with which it dealt, and all were fused into a unity by the spirit of devotion that welled up through all. After prayers he went back to his study, and nothing was heard or seen of him for some hours, except when his heavy tread was heard upstairs as he walked backwards and forwards, or when the strains of what was meant to be a German choral were wafted down from above.

The afternoon he usually spent in visiting, and, so long as he remained in Berwick, there was no more familiar figure in its streets than his. The tall, stalwart form, already a little bent,—but bent, one thought, not so much by the weight of advancing years as by way of making an apology for its height,—the hair already white, the mild and kindly blue eye, the tall hat worn well back on the head, the swallow-tail coat, the swathes within swathes of broad white neckcloth, the umbrella carried, even in the finest weather, under the arm with the handle downward, the gloves in the hands but never on them, the rapid eager stride,—all these come back vividly to those who can remember Berwick in the Sixties and early Seventies of last century. His visitations were still carried out with the method and punctuality which had characterised them in the early days of his ministry, and he usually arranged to make a brief pause for tea with one of the families visited. On these occasions he would frequently be in high spirits, and his hearty and resounding laughter would break out on the smallest provocation. That laugh of his was eminently characteristic of the man. There was nothing smothered or furtive about it; there was not even the vestige of a chuckle in it. Its deep "Ah! hah! hah!" came with a staccato, quacking sound from somewhere low down in the chest, and set his huge shoulders moving in unison with its peals. The whole closed with a long breath of purest enjoyment—a kind of final licking of the lips after the feast was over.

Returning to his house, he always entered it by the back door, apparently because he did not wish to put the servant to the trouble of going upstairs to open the front door for him. It does not seem to have occurred to him to use a latch-key. In the evening there was generally some meeting to go to, but after his return, when evening worship and the invariable supper of porridge and milk were over, he always went back to his study, and its lights were seldom put out until long past midnight.

Although his reading in these solitary hours was of course mainly theological, he always kept fresh his interest in the classical studies of his youth. He did not depend on his communings with Origen and Eusebius for keeping up his Greek, but went back as often as he could find time to Plato and to the Tragedians. Macaulay has defined a Greek scholar as one who can read Plato with his feet on the fender. Dr. Cairns could fully satisfy this condition; indeed he went beyond it, for when he went from home he was in the habit of taking a volume of Plato or Aeschylus with him to read in the train. One of his nephews, at that time a schoolboy, remembers reading with him, when on a holiday visit to Berwick, through the *Alcestis* of Euripides. It may have been because he found it necessary to frighten his young relative into habits of accuracy, or possibly because an outrage committed against a Greek poet was to him the most horrid of all outrages; but anyhow, during these studies, he altogether laid aside that restraint which he was usually so jealous to maintain over his powers of sarcasm and invective. He lay on the study sofa while the lesson was going on, with a Tauchnitz Euripides in his hand; but sometimes, when a false quantity or a more than usually stupid grammatical blunder was made, he would spring to his feet and fairly shout with wrath. Only once had he to consult a Greek lexicon for the meaning of a word; and then it turned out that the meaning he had assigned to it provisionally was the right one. A Latin lexicon he did not possess.

On Sunday, Wallace Green Church was a goodly sight. Forenoon and afternoon, streams of worshippers came pouring by Ravensdowne, Church Street, and Walkergate Lane across the square and into the large building, which was soon filled to overflowing. Then "the Books" were brought in by the stately beadle, and last of all "the Doctor" came hurriedly in, scrambled awkwardly up the pulpit stair, and covered his face with his black gloved hands.15 Then he rose, and in slow monotone gave out the opening psalm, during the singing of which his strong but wandering voice could now and again be distinctly heard above the more artistic strains of the choir and congregation rendering its tribute of praise. The Scripture lessons were read in the same subdued but reverent tones, and the prayers were simple and direct in their language, the emotion that throbbed through them being kept under due restraint. The opening periods of the sermon were pitched in the same note, but when the preacher got fairly into his subject he broke loose from such restraints, and his argument was unfolded, and then massed, and finally pressed home with all the strength of his intellect, reinforced at every stage by the play of his imagination and the glow of a passionate conviction. His "manner" in the pulpit was, it is true, far from graceful. His principal gesture was a jerking of the right arm towards the left shoulder, accompanied sometimes by a bending forward of the upper part of the body; and when he came to his peroration, which he usually delivered with his eyes closed and in lowered tones, he would clasp his hands and move them up and down in front of him. But all these things seemed to fit in naturally to his style of oratory; there was not the faintest trace of affectation in any of them, and, as a matter of fact, they added to the effectiveness of his preaching.

In Wallace Green Dr. Cairns was surrounded by a devoted band of office-bearers and others, who carried on very successful Home Mission work in the town, and kept the various organisations of the church in a vigorous and flourishing state. He had himself no faculty for business details, and he left these mostly to others; but his influence was felt at every point, and operated in a remarkable degree towards the keeping up of the spiritual tone of the church's work. With his elders, who were not merely in regard to ecclesiastical rank, but also in regard to character and ability, the leaders of the congregation, he was always on the most cordial and intimate terms. In numerical strength they usually approximated to the apostolic figure of twelve, and Dr. Cairns used to remark that their Christian names included a surprisingly large number of apostolic pairs. Thus there were amongst them not merely James and John, Matthew and Thomas, but even Philip and Bartholomew.

The Philip here referred to was Dr. Philip Whiteside Maclagan, a brother of the present Archbishop of York and of the late Professor Sir Douglas Maclagan. Dr. Maclagan had been originally an army surgeon, but had been long settled in general practice in Berwick in succession to his father-in-law, the eminent naturalist, Dr. George Johnstone. It was truly said of him that he combined in himself the labours and the graces of Luke the beloved physician and Philip the evangelist. When occasion offered, he would not only diagnose and prescribe but pray at the bedsides of his patients, and his influence was exerted in behalf of everything that was pure and lovely and of good report in the town of Berwick. His delicately chiselled features and fine expression were the true index of a devout and beautiful soul within. Dr. Cairns and he were warmly attached to one another, and he was his minister's right-hand man in everything that concerned the good of the congregation.

It will readily be believed that Dr. Cairns had not been suffered to remain in Berwick during all these years without strong efforts being made to induce him to remove to larger spheres of labour. As a matter of fact, he received in all some half-dozen calls during the course of his ministry from congregations in Edinburgh and Glasgow; while at one period of his life scarcely a year passed without private overtures being made to him which, if he had given any encouragement to them, would have issued in calls. These overtures he in every case declined at once; but when congregations, in spite of him or without having previously consulted him, took the responsibility of proceeding to a formal call, he never intervened to arrest their action. He had a curious respect for the somewhat cumbrous and slow-moving Presbyterian procedure, and when it had been set in motion he felt that it was his duty to let it take its course.

Once when a call to him was in process which he had in its initial stages discouraged, and which he knew that he could not accept, his sister, who had set her heart on furnishing an empty bedroom in the manse at Berwick, was peremptorily bidden to stay her hand lest he might thereby seem to be prejudging that which was not yet before him. Two of the calls he received deserve separate mention. One was in 1855 from Greyfriars Church, Glasgow, at that time the principal United Presbyterian congregation in the city. All sorts of influences were brought to bear upon him to accept it, and for a time he was in grave doubt as to whether it might not be his duty to do so. But two considerations especially decided him to remain in Berwick. One was the state of his health, which was not at that time very good; and the other was the pathetic one, that he wanted to write that book which was never to be written.

Nine years later, in 1864, a yet more determined attempt was made to secure him for Edinburgh. A new congregation had been formed at Morningside, one of the southern suburbs of the city, and it was thought that this would offer a sphere of work and of influence worthy of his powers. A call was accordingly addressed to him, and it was backed up by representations of an almost unique character and weight. The Free Church leaders, with whom he was then brought into close touch by the Union negotiations, urged him to come to Edinburgh. A memorial, signed by one hundred and sixty-seven United Presbyterian elders in the city, told him that, in the interests of their Church, it was of the utmost importance that he should do so. Another memorial, signed by several hundred students at the University, put the matter from their point of view. A still more remarkable document was the following:—

"The subscribers, understanding that the Rev. Dr. Cairns has received a call to the congregation of Morningside, desire to express their earnest and strong conviction that his removal to Edinburgh would be a signal benefit to vital religion throughout Scotland, and more especially in the metropolis, where his great intellectual powers, his deep and wide scholarship, his mastery of the literature of modern unbelief, and the commanding simplicity and godly sincerity of his personal character and public teaching, would find an ample field for their full and immediate exercise."

This was signed (amongst others) by three Judges of the Court of Session, by the Lord Advocate, by the Principal and seven of the Professors of the University, and by such distinguished ministers and citizens as Dr. Candlish, Dr. Hanna, Dr. Lindsay Alexander, Adam Black, Dr. John Brown, and Charles Cowan. It was a remarkable tribute (Adam Black in giving his name said, "This is more than ever was done for Dr. Chalmers"), and it made a deep impression on Dr. Cairns. The Wallace Green congregation, however, sought to counteract it by an argument which amusingly shows how well they knew their man. They appealed to that strain of anxious conscientiousness in him which he had inherited from his father, by urging that all these memorials were "irregular," and that therefore he had no right to consider them in coming to his decision. They also undertook to furnish him with the means of devoting more time to theological study than had hitherto been at his disposal. After a period of hesitation, more painful and prolonged than he had ever passed through on any similar occasion, he decided to remain in Berwick. He was moved to this decision, partly by his attachment to his congregation; partly by a feeling that he could do more for the cause of Union by remaining its minister than would be possible amid the labours of a new city charge; and partly by the hope, which was becoming perceptibly fainter and more wistful, that he might at last find leisure in Berwick to write his book.

But, although he did not become a city minister, he preached very frequently in Edinburgh and Glasgow, and indeed all over the country. His services were in constant request for the opening of churches and on anniversary occasions. He records that in the course of a single year he preached or spoke away from home (of course mostly on week days) some forty or fifty times. Wherever he went he attracted large crowds, on whom his rugged natural eloquence produced a deep impression. It has been recorded that on one occasion, while a vast audience to which he had been preaching in an Edinburgh church was dispersing, a man was overheard expressing his admiration to his neighbour in language more enthusiastic than proper: "He's a deevil o' a preacher!"

With all this burden of work pressing on him, it was a relief when the annual holiday came round and he could get away from it. But this holiday, too, was usually of a more or less strenuous character, and embraced large tracts of country either at home or, more frequently, on the Continent. On these tours his keen human interest asserted itself. He loved to visit places associated with great historic events, or that suggested to him reminiscences of famous men and women. And the actual condition of the people, how they lived, and what they were thinking about, interested him deeply. He spoke to everybody he met, in the train, in the steamboat, or in hotels, in fluent if rather "bookish" German, in correct but somewhat halting French, or, if it was a Roman Catholic priest he had to deal with, in sonorous Latin. And, without anything approaching cant or officiousness, he always tried to bring the conversation round to the subject of religion—to the state of religion in the country in which he was travelling, about which he was always anxious to gain first-hand information, and, if possible and he could do it without offence, to the personal views and experiences of those with whom he conversed. He rarely or never did give offence in this respect, for there was never anything aggressive or clamorous or prying in his treatment of the subject.

On his return to Berwick his congregation usually expected him to give them a lecture on what he had seen, and the MSS. of several of these lectures, abounding in graphic description and in shrewd and often humorous observation of men and things, have been preserved. It must suffice here to give an extract from one of them on a tour in the West of Ireland in 1864, illustrating as it does a curious phase of Irish social life at that time. Dr. Cairns and a small party of friends had embarked in a little steamer on one of the Irish lakes, and were taking note of the gentlemen's seats, varied with occasional ruins, which were coming in view on both sides.

"A fine ancient castle," he goes on to say, "surrounded by trees and almost overhanging the lough, attracted our gaze for some time ere we passed it. The owner's name and character were naturally brought under review. 'Is not Sir —— a Sunday man?' says one of the company to another. 'He is.' The distinction was new to me, and I inferred something good, perhaps some unusual zeal for Sabbath observance or similar virtue. But, alas! for the vanity of human judgments. A 'Sunday man' in the West of Ireland is one who only appears on the Sunday outside his own dwelling, because on any other day he would be arrested for debt. Even on a week day he is safe if he keeps to his own house, where in Ireland, as in England, no writ can force its way. Sir —— was also invulnerable while sitting on the grand jury, where quite lately he had protracted the business to an inordinate length in order to extend his own liberty. As the boat passed close beside his castle, a handsome elderly gentleman appeared at an open window, and with hat in hand and a charming smile on his face made us a most profound and graceful salutation. We could not be insensible to so much courtesy—since it was Sir —— himself who thus welcomed us; but as we waved our hats in reply, one of our party, who had actually a writ out against the fine old Irish gentleman at the very time, with very little prospect of execution, muttered something between his teeth and pressed his hat firmer down on his head than usual. Such landlordism is still not uncommon. The same friend is familiar with writs against other gentlemen whose house is their castle, and to whom Sunday is 'the light of the week.'"

The closing period of Dr. Cairns's ministry at Berwick was made memorable by a remarkable religious revival in the town. Following on a brief visit in January 1874 from Messrs. Moody and Sankey, who had then just closed their first mission in Edinburgh, a movement began which lasted nearly two years. With some help from outside it was carried on during that time mostly by the ministers of the town, assisted by laymen from the various churches, among whom Dr. Maclagan occupied a foremost place. Dr. Cairns threw himself into this movement with ardour, and although he did not intend it, and probably was not aware of it, he was its real leader, giving it at once the impetus and the guidance which it needed. Besides being present, and taking some part whenever he was at home in the crowded evangelistic meetings that for a while were held nightly, and in the prayer-meeting, attended by from one hundred and fifty to two hundred, which met every day at noon, he must have conversed with hundreds of people seeking direction on religious matters during the early months of 1874. And, knowing that many would shrink from the publicity of an Inquiry Meeting, he made a complete canvass of his own congregation, in the course of which by gentle and tactful means he found out those who really desired to be spoken to, and spoke to them. The results of the movement proved to be lasting, and were, in his opinion, wholly good. His own congregation profited greatly by it, and on the Sunday before one of the Wallace Green Communions, in 1874, a great company of young men and women were received into the fellowship of the Church. The catechumens filled several rows of pews in the front of the spacious area of the building, and, when they rose in a body to make profession of their faith, the scene is described as having been most impressive. Specially impressive also must have sounded the words which he always used on such occasions: "You have to-day fulfilled your baptism vow by taking upon yourselves the responsibilities hitherto discharged by your parents. It is an act second only in importance to the private surrender of your souls to God, and not inferior in result to your final enrolment among the saints.... Nothing must separate you from the Church militant till you reach the Church triumphant."

CHAPTER IX

THE PROFESSOR

It had all along been felt that Dr. Cairns must sooner or later find scope for his special powers and acquirements in a professor's chair. In the early years of his ministry he received no fewer than four offers of philosophical professorships, which his views of the ministry and of his consecration to it constrained him to set aside. Three similar offers of theological chairs, the acceptance of which did not involve the same interference with the plan of his life, came to him later, but were declined on other grounds. When, however, a vacancy in the Theological Hall of his own Church occurred by the death of Professor Lindsay, in 1866, the universal opinion in the Church was that it must be filled by him and by nobody else. Dr. Lindsay had been Professor of Exegesis, but the United Presbyterian Synod in May 1867 provided for this subject being dealt with otherwise, and instituted a new chair of Apologetics with a special view to Dr. Cairns's recognised field of study. To this chair the Synod summoned him by acclamation, and, having accepted its call, he began his new work in the following August.

As in his own student days, the Hall met for only two months in each year, and the professors therefore did not need to give up their ministerial charges. So he remained in Berwick, where his congregation were very proud of the new honour that had come to their minister, and that was in some degree reflected on them. Instead of "the Doctor" they now spoke of him habitually as "the Professor," and presented him with a finely befrogged but somewhat irrelevant professor's gown for use in the pulpit at Wallace Green.

Dr. Cairns prepared two courses of lectures for his students—one on the History of Apologetics, and the other on Apologetics proper, or Christian Evidences. For the former, his desire to go to the sources and to take nothing at second-hand led him to make a renewed and laborious study of the Fathers, who were already, to a far greater extent than with most theologians, his familiar friends. His knowledge of later controversies, such as that with the Deists, which afterwards bore fruit in his work on "Unbelief in the Eighteenth Century," was also widened and deepened at this time. These historical lectures were almost overweighted by the learning which he thus accumulated; but they were at once massive in their structure and orderly and lucid in their arrangement.

In the other course, on Christian Evidences, he did not include any discussion on Theism which—probably because of his special familiarity with the Deistical and kindred controversies, and also because the modern assaults on supernatural Christianity from the Evolutionary and Agnostic standpoint had not yet become pressing—he postulated. And, discarding the traditional division of the Evidences into Internal and External, he classified them according to their relation to the different Attributes of God, as manifesting His Power, Knowledge, Wisdom, Holiness, and Benignity. With this course he incorporated large parts of his unfinished treatise on "The Difficulties of Christianity," which, after he had thus broken it up, passed finally out of sight.

The impression which he produced on his students by these lectures, and still more by his personality, was very great. "I suppose," writes one of them, "no men are so hypercritical as students after they have been four or five years at the University. To those who are aware of this, it will give the most accurate impression of our feeling towards Dr. Cairns when I say that, with regard to him, criticism could not be said to exist. We all had for him an appreciation which was far deeper than ordinary admiration; it was admiration blended with loyalty and veneration."[16] Specially impressive were the humility which went along with his gifts and learning, and the wide charity which made him see good in everything. One student's appreciation of this latter quality found whimsical expression in a cartoon which was delightedly passed from hand to hand in the class, and which represented Dr. Cairns cordially shaking hands with the Devil. A "balloon" issuing from his mouth enclosed some such legend as this: "I hope you are very well, sir. I am delighted to make your acquaintance, and to find that you are not nearly so black as you are painted."

During the ten years' negotiations for Union a considerable number of pressing reforms in the United Presbyterian Church were kept back from fear of hampering the negotiations, and because it was felt that such matters might well be postponed to be dealt with in a United Church. But, when the negotiations were broken off, the United Presbyterians, having recovered their liberty of action, at once began to set their house in order. One of the first matters thus taken up was the question of Theological Education. As has been already mentioned, the theological curriculum extended over five sessions of two months. It was now proposed to substitute for this a curriculum extending over three sessions of five months, as being more in accordance with the requirements of the times and as bringing the Hall into line with the Universities and the Free Church Colleges. A scheme, of which this was the leading feature, was finally adopted by the Synod in May 1875. It necessarily involved the separation of the professors from their charges, and accordingly the Synod addressed a call to Dr. Cairns to leave Berwick and become Professor of Systematic Theology and Apologetics in the newly constituted Hall, or, as it was henceforth to be designated—"College." In this chair it was proposed that he should have as his colleague the venerable Dr. Harper, who was the senior professor in the old Hall, and who was now appointed the first Principal of the new College.

Dr. Cairns had thus to make his choice between his congregation and his professorship, and, with many natural regrets, he decided in favour of the latter. This decision, which he announced to his people towards the close of the summer, had the incidental effect of keeping him in the United Presbyterian Church, for in the following year the English congregations of that Church were severed from the parent body to form part of the new Presbyterian Church of England; and Wallace Green congregation, somewhat against its will, and largely in response to Dr. Cairns's wishes, went with the rest. He had still a year to spend in Berwick, broken only by the last session of the old Hall in August and September, and that year he spent in quiet, steady, and happy work. In June 1876 he preached his farewell sermon to an immense and deeply moved congregation from the words (Rom. i. 16), "I am not ashamed of the gospel of Christ: for it is the power of God unto salvation unto every one that believeth." "For more than thirty years," he concluded, "I have preached this gospel among you, and I bless His name this day that to not a few it has by His grace proved the power of God unto salvation. To Him I ascribe all the praise; and I would rather on such an occasion remember defects and shortcomings than dwell even upon what He has wrought for us. The sadness of parting from people to whom I have been bound by such close and tender ties, from whom I have received every mark of respect, affection, and encouragement, and in regard to whom I feel moved to say, 'If I forget thee, O Jerusalem, let my right hand forget her cunning,' inclines me rather to self-examination and to serious fear lest any among you should have suffered through my failure to set forth and urge home this gospel of salvation. If then any of you should be in this case, through my fault or your own, that you have not yet obeyed the gospel of Christ, I address to you in Christ's name one parting call that you may at length receive the truth."

A few weeks later he and his sister removed to Edinburgh, where they were joined in the autumn by their brother William. William Cairns, who had been schoolmaster at Oldcambus for thirty-two years, was in many respects a notable man. Deprived, as we have seen, in early manhood of the power of walking, he had set himself to improve his mind and had acquired a great store of general information. He was shrewd, humorous, genial, and intensely human, and had made himself the centre of a large circle of friends, many of whom were to be found far beyond the bounds of his native parish and county. Since his mother's death an elder sister had kept house for him, but she had died in the previous winter, and at his brother's urgent request he had consented to give up his school al Oldcambus and make his home for the future with him in Edinburgh. The house No. 10 Spence Street, in which for sixteen years the brothers and sister lived together, is a modest semi-detached villa in a short street running off the Dalkeith Road, in one of the southern suburbs of the city. It had two great advantages in Dr. Cairns's eyes—one being that it was far enough away from the College to ensure that he would have a good walk every day in going there and back; and the other, that its internal arrangements were very convenient for his brother finding his way in his wheel-chair about it, and out of it when he so desired.

The study, as at Berwick, was upstairs, and was a large lightsome room, from which a view of the Craigmillar woods, North Berwick Law, and even the distant Lammermoors, could be obtained—a view which was, alas! soon blocked up by the erection of tall buildings. At the back of the house, downstairs, was the sitting-room, where the family meals were taken and where William sat working at his desk. He had been fortunate enough to secure, almost immediately after his arrival in Edinburgh, a commission from Messrs. A. & C. Black to prepare the Index to the ninth edition of the *Encyclopaedia Britannica*, then in course of publication. During the twelve years that the work lasted he performed the possibly unique feat of reading through the whole of the twenty-five volumes of the Encyclopaedia, and thus added considerably to his already encyclopaedic stock of miscellaneous information. Opening off the sitting-room was a smaller room, or rather a large closet, commanding one of the finest views in Edinburgh of the lion-shaped Arthur's Seat; and here of an evening he would sit in his chair alone, or surrounded by the friends who soon began to gather about him,

"And smoke, yea, smoke and smoke."

Sometimes a more than usually resounding peal of laughter would bring the professor down from his study to find out what was the matter, and to join in the merriment; and then, after a few hearty words of greeting to the visitors, he would plead the pressure of his work and return to the company of Justin or Evagrius.

His three nephews, who during the Edinburgh period were staying in town studying for the ministry, always spent Saturday afternoon at Spence Street, and sometimes a student friend would come with them. Dr. Cairns was usually free on such occasions to devote an hour or two to his young friends. He was always ready to enter into discussions on philosophical problems that happened to be interesting them, and the power and ease with which he dealt with these gave an impression as of one heaving up and pitching about huge masses of rock. His part in these discussions commonly in the end became a monologue, which he delivered lying back in his chair, with his shoulders resting on the top bar of it, and which he sometimes accompanied with the peculiar jerk of his right arm habitual to him in preaching. A *snell* remark of his brother William suggesting some new and comic association with a philosophic term dropped in the course of the discussion, would bring him back with a roar of laughter to the actual world and to more sublunary themes. When the young men rose to leave he always accompanied them to the front door, and bade each of them good-bye with a hearty "Πάντα τὰ καλά σοι γένοιτο," 17 [Greek: Panta ta kala soi genoito] and an invariable injunction to "put your foot on it,"—"it" being the spring catch by which the gate was opened.

Once a week during the session a party of six or eight students came to tea at Spence Street, until the whole of his two classes had been gone over. After tea in the otherwise seldom used dining-room of the house, some of the party accompanied the professor to the study. Here he would show them his more treasured volumes, such as his first edition of Butler, which he would tell them he made a point of reading through once a year. Others, who preferred a less unclouded atmosphere, withdrew with his brother into his sanctum. Soon all reassembled in the dining-room, and a number of hymns were sung—some of Sankey's, which were then in everybody's mouth, some of his favourite German hymns with their chorals, which might suggest references to his student days in Berlin or to later experiences in the Fatherland, and some by the great English hymn-writers. At last came family worship, always impressive as conducted by him, but often the most memorable feature by far in these gatherings. It was a very simple, and may seem a very humdrum, way of spending an evening; but the homely hospitality of the household—the conversational gifts, very different in kind as these were, of himself and his brother—and, above all, his genial and benignant presence, made everything go off well, and the students went away with a deepened veneration for their professor now that they had seen him in his own house.

During his first two years in Edinburgh he was busily engaged in writing lectures and in adapting his existing stock to the requirements of the new curriculum. Of these lectures, and of others which he wrote in later years, it must be said that, while all of them were the fruit of conscientious and strenuous toil, they were of unequal merit, or at least of unequal effectiveness. Some of them, particularly in his Apologetic courses, were brilliant and stimulating. Whenever he had a great personality to deal with, such as Origen, Grotius, or Pascal, or, in a quite different way, Voltaire, he rose to the full height of his powers. His criticisms of Hume, of Strauss, and of Renan, were also in their own way masterly. But a course which he had on Biblical Theology seemed to be hampered by a too rigid view of Inspiration, which did not allow him to lay sufficient stress on the different types of doctrine corresponding to the different individualities of the writers. And when, after the death of Principal Harper, he took over the entire department of Systematic Theology, his lectures on this, the "Queen of sciences," while full of learning and sometimes rising to grandeur, gave one on the whole a sense of incompleteness, even of fragmentariness. This impression was deepened by the oral examinations which he was in the habit of holding every week on his lectures.

For these examinations he prepared most carefully, sitting up sometimes till two o'clock in the morning collecting material and verifying references which he deemed necessary to make them complete. His aim in them was not only to test the students' attention and progress, but to communicate information of a supplementary and miscellaneous character which he had been unable to work into his lectures. And so he would bring down to the class a tattered Father or two, and would regale its members with long Greek quotations and with a mass of details that were pure gold to him but were hid treasure to them. His examination of individual students was lenient in the extreme. It used to be said of him that if he asked a question to which the correct answer was Yes, while the answer he got was No, he would exert his ingenuity to show that in a certain subtle and hitherto unsuspected sense the real answer *was* No, and that Mr. So-and-so deserved credit for having discovered this, and for having boldly dared to *say* No at the risk of being misunderstood. This, of course, is caricature; but it nevertheless sufficiently indicates his general attitude to his students.

It was the same with the written as with the oral examinations. In these he assigned full marks to a large proportion of the papers sent in. Once it was represented to him that this method of valuation prevented his examination results from having any influence on the adjudication of a prize that was given every year to the student who had the highest aggregate of marks in all the classes. He admitted the justice of this contention, and promised to make a change. When he announced the results of his next examination it was found that he had been as good as his word; but the change consisted in this: that whereas formerly two-thirds of the class had received full marks, now two-thirds of the class received ninety per cent.!

And yet the popular idea of his inability to distinguish between a good student and a bad one was quite wrong. He was not so simple as he seemed. All who have sat in his classroom remember times when a sudden keen look from him showed that he knew quite well when liberties were being attempted with him, and gave rise to the uncomfortable suspicion that, as it was put, "he could see more things with his eyes shut than most men could see with theirs wide open." The fact is, that all his leniency with his students, and all his apparent ascription to them of a high degree of diligence, scholarship, and mental grasp, had their roots not in credulity but in charity—the charity which "believeth all things, hopeth all things, endureth all things." His very defects came from an excess of charity, and one loved him all the better because of them. Hence it came about that his students got far more from contact with his personality than they got from his teaching. It is not so much his lectures as his influence that they look back to and that they feel is affecting them still.

When Dr. Cairns came to Edinburgh from Berwick, it was only to a limited extent that he allowed himself to take part in public work outside that which came to him as a minister and Professor of Theology. There were, however, two public questions which interested him deeply, and the solution of which he did what he could by speech and influence to further. One of these was the question of Temperance. During the first twenty years of his ministry he had not felt called upon to take up any strong position on this question, although personally he had always been one of the most abstemious of men. But about the year 1864 he had, without taking any pledge or enrolling himself on the books of any society, given up the use of alcohol. He had done so largely as an experiment—to see whether his influence would thereby be strengthened with those in his own congregation and beyond it whom he wished to reclaim from intemperance.

When he became a professor he was invited to succeed Dr. Lindsay as President of the Students' Total Abstinence Society, and, as no absolute pledge was exacted from the members, he willingly agreed to do so. From this time his influence was more and more definitely enlisted on behalf of Total Abstinence, and in 1874 he took a further step. In trying to save from intemperance a friend in Berwick who was not a member of his own congregation, he urged him to join the Good Templars, at that time the only available society of total abstainers in the town. In order to strengthen his friend's hands, he agreed to join along with him. This step happily proved to be successful as regarded its original purpose, and Dr. Cairns remained a Good Templar during the rest of his life.

While there were some things about the Order that did not appeal to him, such as the ritual, the "regalia," and the various grades of membership and of office, with their mysterious initials, he looked upon these things as non-essentials, and was in hearty sympathy with its general principles and work. But, although he was often urged to do so, he never would accept office nor advance beyond the initiatory stage of membership represented by the simple white "bib" of infancy. On coming to Edinburgh, he looked about for a Lodge to connect himself with, and ultimately chose one of the smallest and most obscure in the city. The members consisted chiefly of men and women who had to work so late that the hour of meeting could not be fixed earlier than 9 p.m. He was present at these meetings as often as he could, and only lamented that he could not attend more frequently.

While fully recognising the right of others to come to a different conclusion from his own, and while uniformly basing his total abstinence on the ground of Christian expediency and not on that of absolute Divine law, his view of it as a Christian duty grew clearer every year. And he carried his principles out rigidly wherever he went. He perplexed German waiters by his elaborate explanations as to why he drank no beer; and once, as he came down the Rhine, he had a characteristically sanguine vision of the time when the vineyards on its banks would only be used for the production of raisins. At the same time his interest in Temperance work, alike in its religious, social, and political aspects, was always becoming keener. He was frequently to be found on Temperance platforms, and was in constant request for the preaching of Temperance sermons. Some of his speeches and sermons on the question have been reprinted and widely read, and one New Year's tract which he wrote has had a circulation of one hundred and eighty thousand.

The other question in which he took a special interest was that of Disestablishment. To those who adopted the "short and easy method" of accounting for the Disestablishment movement in Scotland by saying that it was all due to jealousy and spite on the part of its promoters, his adhesion to that movement presented a serious difficulty. For no one could accuse him of jealousy or spite. Hence it was a favourite expedient to represent him as the tool of more designing men—as one whose simplicity had been imposed upon, and who had been thrust forward against his better judgment to do work in which he had no heart. This theory is not only entirely groundless, but entirely unnecessary; because the action which he took on this question can readily be explained by a reference to convictions he had held all his life, and to circumstances which seemed to him to call for their assertion.

He had been a Voluntary ever since he had begun to think on such questions. His father, in the days of his boyhood, had subscribed, along with a neighbour, for the *Voluntary Church Magazine,* and the subject had often been discussed in the cottage at Dunglass. It will be remembered that during his first session at the University he was an eager disputant with his classmates on the Voluntary side, and that towards the close of his course, after a memorable debate in the Diagnostic Society, he secured a victory for the policy of severing the connection between Church and State. These views he had never abandoned, and in a lecture on Disestablishment delivered in Edinburgh in 1872 he re-stated them. While admitting, as the United Presbyterian Synod had done in adopting the "Articles of Agreement," that the State ought to frame its policy on Christian lines, he denied that it was its duty or within its competence to establish and endow the Church. This is, to quote his own words, "an overstraining of its province,—a forgetfulness that its great work is civil and not spiritual,—and an encroachment without necessity or call, and indeed, as I believe, in the face of direct Divine arrangements, on the work of the Christian Church."

These, then, being his views, what led him to seek to make them operative by taking part in a Disestablishment campaign? Two things especially. One of these was the activity at that time of a Broad Church party within the Established Church. He maintained that this was no mere domestic concern of that Church, and claimed the right as a citizen to deal with it. In a national institution views were held and taught of which he could not approve, and which he considered compromised him as a member of the nation. He felt he must protest, and he protested thus.

The other ground of his action was the conviction, which recent events had very much strengthened, that the continued existence of an Established Church was the great obstacle to Presbyterian Union in Scotland. It is true that there was nothing in the nature of things to prevent the Free and United Presbyterian Churches coming together in presence of an Established Church. As a matter of fact, they have done so since Dr. Cairns's death, though not without secessions, collective and individual. But experience had shown that it was the existence of an Established Church, towards which the Anti-Union party had turned longing eyes, which was the determining factor in the wrecking of the Union negotiations. Besides, Dr. Cairns looked forward to a wider Union than one merely between the Free and United Presbyterian Churches, and he was convinced that only on the basis of Disestablishment could such a Union take place. To the argument that, if the Church of Scotland were to be disestablished, its members would be so embittered against those who had brought this about that they would decline to unite with them, he was content to reply that that might safely be left to the healing power of time. The petulant threat of some, that in the event of Disestablishment they would abandon Presbyterianism, he absolutely declined to notice.

The Disestablishment movement had been begun before Dr. Cairns left Berwick, and he supported it with voice and pen till the close of his life. He did so, it need not be said, without bitterness, endeavouring to make it clear that his quarrel was with the adjective and not with the substantive—with the "Established" and not with the "Church," and under the strong conviction that he was engaged "in a great Christian enterprise."

CHAPTER X

THE PRINCIPAL

During 1877 and 1878 the United Presbyterian Church was much occupied with a discussion that had arisen in regard to its relation to the "Subordinate Standards," i.e. to the Westminster *Confession of Faith* and the *Larger and Shorter Catechisms*. These formed the official creed of the Church, and assent to them was exacted from all its ministers, probationers, and elders. A change of opinion, perhaps not so much regarding the doctrines set forth in these documents as regarding the perspective in which they were to be viewed, had been manifesting itself with the changing times. It was felt that standards of belief drawn up in view of the needs, reflecting the thought, and couched in the language of the seventeenth century, were not an adequate expression of the faith of the Church in the nineteenth century. The points with regard to which this difficulty was more acutely felt were chiefly in the region of the "Doctrines of Grace"—the Divine Decrees, the Freedom of the Human Will, and the Extent of the Atonement. Accordingly, a movement for greater liberty was set on foot.

There were many, of course, in the Church who had no sympathy with this movement, and who, if they had been properly organised and led, might have been able to defeat it. But the recognised and trusted leaders of the Church were of opinion that the matter must be sympathetically dealt with, and, on the motion of Principal Harper, the Synod of 1877 appointed a Committee to consider it, and to bring up a report. This Committee, of which Dr. Cairns was one of the conveners, soon found that, if relief were to be granted, they had only two alternatives before them. They must deal either with the Creed or with the terms of subscription to it. There were some who urged that an entirely new and much shorter Creed should be drawn up. Dr. Cairns was decidedly opposed to this proposal. The subject of the Creeds of the Reformed Churches was one of his many specialties in the field of Church History, and he had a reverence for those venerable documents, whose articles—so dry and formal to others—suggested to his imagination the centuries of momentous controversy which they summed up, and the great champions of the faith who had borne their part therein. Besides, he was very much alive to the danger of falling out of line with the other Presbyterian Churches in Great Britain and America, who still maintained, in some form or other, their allegiance to the Westminster Standards.

His influence prevailed, and the second alternative was adopted. A "Declaratory Statement" was drawn up of the sense in which, while retaining the Standards, the Church understood them. This Statement dealt with the points above referred to in a way that would, it was thought, give sufficient relief to consciences that had shrunk from the naked rigour of the words of the *Confession*, It also contained a paragraph which secured liberty of opinion on matters "not entering into the substance of the faith," the right of the Church to guard against abuse of this liberty being expressly reserved. Dr. Cairns submitted this "Declaratory Statement" to the Synods of 1878 and 1879, in speeches of notable power and wealth of historic illustration, and, in the latter year, it was unanimously adopted and became a "Declaratory Act." The precedent thus set has been followed by nearly all the Presbyterian Churches which have since then had occasion to deal with the same problem.

Except when he had to expound and recommend some scheme for which he had become responsible, or when he had been laid hold of by others to speak in behalf of a "Report" or a proposal in which they were interested, Dr. Cairns did not intervene often in the debates of the United Presbyterian Synod. He preferred, to the disappointment of many of his friends, to listen rather than to speak, and shrank from putting himself in any way forward. He had been Moderator of the Synod in 1872, and as an ex-Moderator he had the privilege, accorded by custom, of sitting on the platform of the Synod Hall on the benches to the right and left of the chair. But he never seemed comfortable up there. He would sit with his hands pressed together, and in a stooping posture, as if he wanted to make his big body as small and inconspicuous as possible; and, as often as he could, he would go down and take his place among the rank and file of the members far back in the hall. But he had all a true United Presbyterian's loyal affection for the Synod, and a peculiar delight in those reunions of old friends which its meetings afforded. Amongst his oldest friends was William Graham, who although, since the English Union, no longer a United Presbyterian, simply could not keep away from the haunts of his youth when the month of May came round. On such occasions he was always Dr. Cairns's guest at Spence Street. He kept things lively there with his nimble wit, and in particular subjected his host to a perpetual and merciless fire of "chaff." No one else ventured to assail him as Graham thus did; for, with all his geniality and unaffected humility, there was a certain personal dignity about him which few ventured to invade. But he took all his friend's banter with a smile of quiet enjoyment, and sometimes a more than usually outrageous sally would send him into convulsions of laughter, whose resounding peals filled the house with their echoes.

In the spring of 1879 died the venerable Principal Harper. Dr. Cairns felt the loss very keenly, for Dr. Harper had been a loyal and generous friend and colleague, on whose clear and firm judgment he had been wont to rely in many a difficult emergency. Besides, as his biographer has truly said, "he was habitually thankful to have someone near him whom he could fairly ask to take the foremost place."[18] Now that Dr. Harper was gone, there seemed to be no doubt that that foremost place would be thrust upon him. These expectations were fulfilled by the Synod of that year, which unanimously and enthusiastically appointed him Principal of the College. His friend Dr. Graham, who, as a corresponding member from the Synod of the Presbyterian Church of England, supported the appointment, gave voice to the universal feeling when he described him as "a man of thought and labour and love and God, who had one defect which endeared him to them all—that he was the only man who did not know what a rare and noble man he was."

In the following year (1880) Principal Cairns delivered the Cunningham Lectures. These lectures were given on a Free Church foundation, instituted in memory of the distinguished theologian whose name it bears; and now for the first time the lecturer was chosen from beyond the borders of the Free Church. Dr. Cairns highly appreciated the compliment that was thus paid him, regarding it as a happy augury of the Union which he was sure was coming. He had chosen as his subject "Unbelief in the eighteenth century as contrasted with its earlier and later history"; and, although it was one in which he was already at home, he had again worked over the familiar ground with characteristic diligence and thoroughness. Thus, in preparing for one of the lectures, he read through twenty volumes of Voltaire, out of a set of fifty which had been put at his disposal by a friend. The first lecture dealt with Unbelief in the first four centuries, which he contrasted in several respects with that of the eighteenth. Then followed one on the Unbelief of the seventeenth century, then three on the Unbelief of the eighteenth century, in England, France, and Germany respectively; and, finally, one on the Unbelief of the nineteenth century, from whose representatives he selected three for special criticism as typical, viz. Strauss, Renan, and John Stuart Mill. These lectures, while not rising to the level of greatness, impress one with his mastery of the immense literature of the subject, and are characterised throughout by lucidity of arrangement and by sobriety and fairness of judgment. They were very well received when they were delivered, and were favourably reviewed when they were published a year later.[19]

Between the delivery and the publication of the Cunningham Lectures Dr. Cairns spent five months in the United States and Canada. The immediate object of this American tour was to fulfil an engagement to be present at the Philadelphia meeting of the General Council of the Presbyterian Alliance—an organisation in which he took the deepest interest, as it was in the line of his early aspirations after a great comprehensive Presbyterian Union. But he arranged his tour so as to enable him also to be present at the General Assembly of the American Presbyterian Church at Madison, and at that of the Presbyterian Church of Canada at Montreal. The rest of the time at his disposal he spent in lengthened excursions to various scenes of interest. He visited the historic localities of New England and crossed the continent to San Francisco, stopping on the way at Salt Lake City, and extending his journey to the Yo-Semite Valley. More than once he went far out of his way to seek out an old friend or the relative of some member of his Berwick congregation. Wherever he went he preached,—in fact every Sunday of these five months, including those he spent on the Atlantic, was thus occupied,—and everywhere his preaching and his personality made a deep impression. As regarded himself, he used to say that this American visit "lifted him out of many ruts" and gave him new views of the vitality of Christianity and new hopes for its future developments.

After the publication of the Cunningham Lectures there was a widely cherished hope that Dr. Cairns would produce something still more worthy of his powers and his reputation. He was now free from the incessant engagements of an active ministry, and he had by this time got his class lectures well in hand. But, although the opportunity had come, the interest in speculative questions had sensibly declined. There is an indication of this in the Cunningham Lectures themselves. In the last of these, as we have seen, he had selected Mill as the representative of English nineteenth-century Unbelief. Even then Mill was out of date; but Mill was the last British thinker whose system he had thoroughly mastered. In the index to his *Life and Letters* the names of Darwin and Herbert Spencer do not occur, and even in an Apologetic tract entitled *Is the Evolution of Christianity from mere Natural Sources Credible?* which he wrote in 1887 for the Religious Tract Society, there is no reference whatever to any writer of the Evolutionary School. With his attitude to later German theological literature it is somewhat different, for here he tried to keep himself abreast of the times. Yet even here the books that interested him most were mainly historical, such as the first volume of Ritschl's great work on Justification (almost the only German book he read in a translation), and the three volumes of Harnack's *History of Dogma*.

This decay of interest in speculative thought might be attributed to the decline of mental freshness and of hospitality to new ideas which often comes with advancing years, were it not that, in his case, there was no such decline. On the contrary, as his interest in speculative thought gradually withered, his interest on the side of scholarship and linguistics became greater than ever, and his energy here was always seeking new outlets for itself. When he was nearly sixty he began the study of Assyrian. He did so in connection with his lectures on Apologetics,—because he wanted to give his class some idea of the confirmation of the Scripture records, which he believed were to be found in the cuneiform inscriptions. But ere long the study took possession of him. His letters, and the little time-table diary of his daily studies, record the hours he devoted to it. When he went to America he took his Assyrian books with him, and pored over them on the voyage whenever the Atlantic would allow him to do so. And he was fully convinced that what interested him so intensely must interest his students too. One of them, the Rev. J.H. Leckie, thus describes how he sought to make them share in his enthusiasm:—

"One day when we came down to the class, we found the blackboard covered with an Assyrian inscription written out by himself before lecture hour, and the zest, the joy with which he discoursed upon the strange figures and signs showed that, though white of hair and bent in frame, he was in the real nature of him very young. For two days he lectured on this inscription with the most assured belief that we were following every word, and there was deep regret in his face and in his voice when he said, 'And now, gentlemen, I am afraid we must return to our theology.'"[20]

Another of his students, referring to the same lectures, writes as follows:—

"It was fine, and one loves him all the more for it, but it was exasperating too, with such tremendous issues at stake in the world of living thought, to see him pounding away at those truculent old Red Indians in their barbarian original tongue. Yet I would not for much forget those days when we saw him escaping utterly from all worries and troubles and perfectly happy before a blackboard covered with amazing characters. It was pure innocent delight in a new world of knowledge, like a child's in a new story-book."

When he was sixty-three he added Arabic to his other acquirements. It is not quite clear whether he had in view any purpose in connection with his professional work beyond the desire to know the originals of all the authorities quoted in his lectures. But, when he had sufficiently mastered the language to be able to read the Koran, he knew that he had two grounds for self-congratulation, and these were sufficiently characteristic. One was that he had his revenge on Gibbon, who had described so triumphantly the career of the Saracens and who yet had not known a word of their language. The other was that he was now able to pray in Arabic for the conversion of the Mohammedans.

About the same time he began to learn Dutch. He assigned as one reason for this that he wanted to read Kuenen's works. But as the only one of these that he had was in his library already, having come to him from the effects of a deceased friend, it is possible that this was just an unconscious excuse on his part for indulging in the luxury of learning a new language— that he read Kuenen in order to learn Dutch, instead of learning Dutch in order to read Kuenen. However, his knowledge of the language enabled him to follow closely a movement which excited his interest in no common degree, viz. the secession of a large evangelical party from the rationalistic State Church of Holland, under Abraham Kuyper, the present Prime Minister of that country, and their organisation into a Free Presbyterian Church.

Other languages at which he worked during this period were Spanish, of which he acquired the rudiments during his tour in California; and Dano-Norwegian, which he picked up during a month's residence at Christiania in 1877, and furbished for a meeting of the Evangelical Alliance at Copenhagen in 1884. All this time he was pursuing his Patristic and other historical studies with unflagging vigour, always writing new lectures, always maintaining his love of abstract knowledge and his eager desire to add to his already vast stores of learning. When, a year and a half before his death, a vacancy occurred in the Church History chair in the College, he stepped into the breach and delivered a course of lectures on the Fathers, which took his class by storm.

"His manner," says one who heard these lectures, "was quite different in the Church History classroom from what it was in that of Systematic Theology. In the latter he taught like a man who felt wearied and old; but in the former he showed a surprising freshness and enthusiasm. It was delightful to see him in the Church History class forgetting age and care, and away back in spirit with Origen and his other old friends."

These lectures, while abounding in searching and masterly criticism of doctrinal views, are specially noticeable for their delineation of the living power of Christianity as exhibited in the men and the times with which they deal. This was the aspect of Christian truth which had all along attracted him. It was what had determined his choice of the ministry as the main work of his life, and in his later years it still asserted its power over him. Although he had now no longer a ministerial charge of his own, he could not separate himself from the active work of the Church—he could not withdraw from contact with the Christian life which it manifested.

During the winter months he preached a good deal in Edinburgh, especially by way of helping young or weak congregations, more than one of which he had at different times under his immediate care until they had been lifted out of the worst of their difficulties. In summer he ranged over the whole United Presbyterian Church from Shetland to Galloway, preaching to great gatherings wherever he went. In arranging these expeditions, he always gave the preference to those applications which came to him from poor, outlying, and sparsely peopled districts, where discouragements were greatest and the struggle to "maintain ordinances" was most severe. His visits helped to lift the burden from many a weary back, and never failed to leave happy and inspiring memories behind them. Among these summer engagements he always kept a place for his old congregation at Berwick, which he regularly visited in the month of June, preaching twice in the church on Sunday, and finishing the day's work by preaching again from the steps of the Town Hall in the evening. On these occasions the broad High Street, at the foot of which the Town Hall stands, was always crowded from side to side and a long way up its course, while all the windows within earshot were thrown open and filled with eager listeners.

In this continual pursuit of knowledge, and in the contemplation, whether in history or in the world around him, of Christianity as a Life, his main interests more and more lay. In the one we can trace the influence of Hamilton, in the other perhaps that of Neander—the two teachers of his youth who had most deeply impressed him. Relatively to these, Systematic Theology, and even Apologetics, receded into the background. Secure in his "*aliquid inconcussum*," he came increasingly to regard the life of the individual Christian and the collective life of the Church as the most convincing of all witnesses to the Unseen and the Supernatural.

Meanwhile the apologetic of his own life was becoming ever more impressive. In the years 1886 and 1887 he lost by death several of his dearest friends. In the former year died Dr. W.B. Robertson of Irvine; and, later, Dr. John Ker, who had been his fellow-student at the University and at the Divinity Hall, his neighbour at Alnwick in the early Berwick days, and at last his colleague as a professor in the United Presbyterian College. In the early part of the following year his youngest sister, Agnes, who with her husband, the Rev. J.C. Meiklejohn, had come to live in Edinburgh two years before for the better treatment of what proved to be a mortal disease, passed away. And in the autumn he lost the last and the dearest of the friends that had been left to him in these later years, William Graham. These losses brought him yet closer than he had been before to the unseen and eternal world.

He was habitually reticent about his inner life and his habits of devotion. No one knew his times of prayer or how long they lasted. Once, indeed, his simplicity of character betrayed him in regard to this matter. The door of his retiring-room at the College was without a key, and he would not give so much trouble as to ask for one. So, in order that he might be quite undisturbed, he piled up some forms and chairs against the door on the inside, forgetting entirely that the upper part of it was obscure glass and that his barricade was perfectly visible from without. It need not be said that no one interrupted him or interfered with his belief that he had been unobserved by any human eye. But it did not require an accidental disclosure like this to reveal the fact that he spent much time in prayer. No one who knew him ever so little could doubt this, and no one could hear him praying in public without feeling sure that he had learned how to do it by long experience in the school of private devotion.

Purified thus by trial and nourished by prayer, his character went on developing and deepening. His humility, utterly unaffected, like everything else about him, became if possible more marked. He was not merely willing to take the lowest room, but far happiest when he was allowed to take it. In one of his classes there was a blind student, and, when a written examination came on, the question arose, How was he to take part in it? Principal Cairns offered to write down the answers to the examination questions to his student's dictation, and it was only after lengthened argument and extreme reluctance on his part that he was led to see that the authorities would not consent to this arrangement.

It was the same with his charity. He was always putting favourable constructions on people's motives and believing good things of them, even when other people could find very little ground for doing so. In all sincerity he would carry this sometimes to amusing lengths. Reference has been made to this already, but the following further illustration of it may be added here. One day, when in company with a friend, the conversation turned on a meeting at which Dr. Cairns had recently been present. At this meeting there was a large array of speakers, and a time limit had to be imposed to allow all of them to be heard. One of the speakers, however, when arrested by the chairman's bell, appealed to the audience, with whom he was getting on extremely well, for more time. Encouraged by their applause, he went on and finished his speech, with the result that some of his fellow-speakers who had come long distances to address the meeting were crushed into a corner, if not crowded out. Dr. Cairns somehow suspected that his friend was going to say something strong about this speaker's conduct, and, before a word could be spoken, rushed to his defence. "He couldn't help himself. He was at the mercy of that shouting audience—a most unmannerly mob!" And then, feeling that he had rather overshot the mark, he added in a parenthetic murmur, "Excellent Christian people they were, no doubt!"

But not the least noticeable thing about him remains to be mentioned— the persistent hopefulness of his outlook. This became always more pronounced as he grew older. Others, when they saw the advancing forces of evil, might tremble for the Ark of God; but he saw no occasion for trembling, and he declined to do so. He was sure that the great struggle that was going on was bound sooner or later, and rather sooner than later, to issue in victory for the cause he loved. And although his great knowledge of the past, and his enthusiasm for the great men who had lived in it, might have been expected to draw his eyes to it with regretful longing, he liked much better to look forward than to look back, using as he did so the words of a favourite motto; "The best is yet to be."

All these qualities found expression in a speech he delivered on the occasion of the presentation of his portrait to the United Presbyterian Synod in May 1888. This portrait had been subscribed for by the ministers and laymen of the Church, and painted by Mr. W.E. Lockhart, R.S.A. The presentation took place in a crowded house, and amid a scene of enthusiasm which no one who witnessed it can ever forget. Principal Cairns concluded a brief address thus: "I have now preached for forty-three years and have been a Professor of Theology for more than twenty, and I find every year how much grander the gospel of the grace of God becomes, and how much deeper, vaster, and more unsearchable the riches of Christ, which it is the function of theology to explore. I have had in this and in other churches a band of ministerial brethren, older and younger, with whom it has been a life-long privilege to be associated; and in the professors a body of colleagues so generous and loving that greater harmony could not be conceived. The congregations to which I have preached have far overpaid my labours; and the students whom I have taught have given me more lessons than many books. I have been allowed many opportunities of mingling with Christians of other lands, and have learned, I trust, something more of the unity in diversity of the creed, 'I believe in the Holy Catholic Church.' In that true Church, founded on Christ's sacrifice and washed in His blood, cheered by its glorious memories and filled with its immortal hopes, I desire to live and die. Life and labour cannot last long with me; but I would seek to work to the end for Christian truth, for Christian missions, and for Christian union. Amidst so many undeserved favours, I would still thank God and take courage, and under the weight of all anxieties and failures, and the shadows of separation from loved friends, I would repeat the confession, which, by the grace of God, time only confirms: '*In Te, Domine, speravi; non confundar in aeternum.*'"

CHAPTER XI

THE END OF THE DAY

In May 1891 the report of an inquiry which had been instituted in the previous year into the working of the United Presbyterian College was submitted to the Synod. The portion of it which referred to Principal Cairns's department, and which was enthusiastically approved, concluded as follows: "The Committee would only add that the whole present inquiry has deepened its sense of the immense value of the services of Dr. Cairns to the College, both as Professor and as Principal, and expresses the hope that he may be long spared to adorn the institution of which he is the honoured head, and the Church of which he is so distinguished a representative." The hope thus expressed was not to be fulfilled.

The specially heavy work of the preceding session—the session in which, as already described, he had undertaken part of the work of the Church History class in addition to the full tale of his own—had overtaxed his strength, and, acting on the advice of Dr. Maclagan and his Edinburgh medical adviser, he had cancelled all his engagements for the summer. Almost immediately after the close of the Synod an old ailment which he had contracted by over-exertion during a holiday tour in Wales reappeared, and yielded only partially to surgical treatment. But he maintained his cheerfulness, and neither he nor his friends had any thought that his work was done. In the month of July he paid a visit to his brother David at Stitchel. He had opened his brother's new church there thirteen years before, and it had come to be a standing engagement, looked forward to by very many in the district, that he should conduct special services every year on the anniversary of that occasion. But these annual visits were very brief, and they were broken into not only by the duties of the Sunday, but by the hospitalities usual in country manses at such times. This time, however, there were no anniversary sermons to be preached; he had come for rest, and there was no need for him to hasten his departure. The weather was lovely, and so were the views over the wide valley of the Tweed to the distant Cheviots. He would sit for hours reading under the great elm-tree in the garden amid the scents of the summer flowers. "I have come in to tell you," he said one day to his sister-in-law, "that this is a day which has wandered out of Paradise." "We younger people," wrote his niece, "came nearer to him than ever before. He was as happy as a child, rejoicing with every increase of strength. He greatly enjoyed my brother Willie's singing, especially songs like Sheriff Nicolson's 'Skye' and Shairp's 'Bush aboon Traquair.' We were astonished to find how familiar he was with all sorts of queer out-of-the-way ballads. Never had we seen him so free from care, so genial and even jubilant."[21] The summer Sacrament took place while he was at Stitchel, and he was able to give a brief address to the communicants from the words, "Ye do shew forth the Lord's death till He come," in a voice that was weak and tremulous, but all the more impressive on that account. One of his brother's elders, a farmer in the neighbourhood whom he had known since his schooldays, had arranged that he should address his work-people in the farmhouse, and to this quiet rural gathering he preached what proved to be his last sermon.

He himself, however, had no idea that this was the case; and when he left Stitchel he did so with the purpose of preparing for the work of another session. But as the autumn advanced and his health did not greatly improve, another consultation of his doctors was held, the result of which was that he was pronounced to be suffering from cardiac weakness, and quite unfit for the work of the coming winter. He at once acquiesced in this verdict, and, with unabated cheerfulness, set himself to bring his lectures into a state that would admit of their being easily read to his classes by two friends who had undertaken this duty. This done, he wrote out in full the Greek texts— some five hundred in all—quoted in his lectures on Biblical Theology. These two tasks kept him busy until about the end of the year 1891, when he began an undertaking which many of his friends had long been urging upon him—the preparation of a volume of his sermons for the press. He selected for this purpose those sermons which he had preached most frequently, and which he had, with few exceptions, originally written for sacramental occasions at Berwick—some of them far back in the old Golden Square days. These he carefully transcribed, altering them where he thought this necessary, and not always, in the opinion of many, improving them in the process.

He found that his strength was not unduly strained when he worked thus six or seven hours a day. But he always, as hitherto, spent one hour daily in reading the Scriptures in the original tongues, in which time he could get through three pages of Hebrew and an indefinite quantity of Greek. There was, however, one change in his habits which had become necessary. He was forbidden by the doctors to study at night. And so, instead of going upstairs in the evening, he remained in the comfortable parlour, where he wrote his letters, talked to his brother and sister, or to visitors as they came in, and regaled himself with light literature. This last consisted sometimes of volumes of the Fathers, but more frequently of the Koran in the original. He would frequently read aloud extracts, translating from the Greek and Latin without ever pausing for a word; as regards the Arabic, he had Sale's translation at hand to help him through a tough passage, but he was always a very proud man when he could find his way out of a difficulty without its aid.

As the winter advanced he felt that it was desirable that he should have another medical opinion, so that, in the event of his further incapacity, the Synod at its approaching meeting might make permanent arrangements for carrying on the work of his chair. On the 19th of February he was examined by Drs. Maclagan, Webster, and G.W. Balfour, who certified that he was "unfit for the discharge of any professional duty." After consulting his relatives, he decided to resign his Professorship and the Principalship of the College, and on the 23rd a letter intimating this intention was drafted and despatched. The committee to which it was sent received it with great regret, and a unanimous feeling found expression that, at anyrate, he should retain the office of Principal. This was echoed from every part of the United Presbyterian Church as soon as the news of his contemplated resignation became known; and in a wider circle adequate utterance was given to the public sympathy and regard.

On the 3rd of March he was able to preside at the annual conversazione of his students, when he was in such genial spirits, and seemed to be so well, that humorous references were made by more than one speaker to his approaching resignation as clearly unnecessary, and indeed preposterous. On the following Saturday he travelled to Galashiels to attend the funeral of his cousin John Murray, whose room he had shared during his first session at the University, and in his prayer at the funeral service he referred in touching terms to the close of their life-long friendship. Returning to Edinburgh, he went to stay till Monday with an old friend, whose house afforded him facilities for attending the communion service at Broughton Place Church next day. For although this church, which he had attended as a student, and of which he had been a member since he came to live in Edinburgh, was more than two miles distant from Spence Street, his Puritan training and convictions with regard to the Sabbath would never allow him to go to it in a cab.

On reaching home next week he resumed his work of transcription, and went on with it till Thursday, when, after taking a short walk, he became somewhat unwell. Next day he felt better, and did some writing in the forenoon; but in the afternoon the illness returned, and he went to bed. In the early hours of next morning, Saturday 12th March, his sister, who was watching beside him, saw that a change was coming, and summoned Mr. and Mrs. David Cairns, who had fortunately arrived the evening before. His brother William, on account of his bodily infirmity, remained below. The end was evidently near, but he was conscious at intervals, and his voice when he spoke was clear and firm. "You are very ill, John," said his brother. "Oh no," he replied, "I feel much better." "But you are in good hands?"

"Yes, in the best of hands." Then his mind began to wander, and he spoke more brokenly: "There is a great battle to fight, but the victory is sure ... God in Christ ... Good men must unite and identify themselves with the cause." "What cause?" asked his brother. "The cause of God," he replied. "If they do so, the victory is sure; otherwise, all is confusion ... I have stated the matter; I leave it with you." Then, after a short pause, he suddenly said, "You go first, I follow." These eminently characteristic words were the last he spoke, and as David knelt and prayed at his bedside death came.

The impression produced on the public mind by his life and character, and called into vivid consciousness by the news of his death, found memorable expression on his funeral day, Thursday 17th March. It had been the original intention of his relatives that the funeral arrangements should be carried out as simply as possible, with a service in Rosehall Church, which was close at hand, for those who desired to attend it, and thereafter a quiet walk down to Echo Bank Cemetery, where he was to rest beside his sister Agnes. It was thought that this would be most in accordance with his characteristic humility and shrinking from all that savoured of display. But the public feeling refused to be satisfied with this idea, and the relatives gave way.

The Synod Hall of the United Presbyterian Church, to which the coffin had been removed in the early part of the day, and which holds three thousand, was crowded to its utmost capacity. The Moderator of Synod presided, and beside him on the platform were the Lord Provost, Magistrates and Council of the city, the Principal and Professors of the University, the Principal and Professors of the New College, and many other dignitaries. In the body of the hall were seated, row behind row, the members of the United Presbyterian Synod, who had come from all parts of the country, drawn by affection as well as veneration for him of whom their Church had been so proud. Along with them was a very large number of ministers of the other Scottish Churches, and representatives of public bodies. The galleries were thronged with the general public. The brief service was of that simple and moving kind with which Presbyterian Scotland is wont to commemorate her dead. There was no funeral oration, and the prayers, which were led by Dr. Macgregor, the Moderator of the Established Church General Assembly, by Principal Rainy, and by Dr. Andrew Thomson, while full of the sense of personal loss, gave expression to the deep thankfulness felt by all present that such a life had been lived, and lived for so long, among them. One incident created a deep impression. After the coffin had been removed, the various representative bodies successively left the hall to take their places in the procession that was being marshalled without. "Wallace Green Church, Berwick" was called. Then a great company of men rose to their feet, showing that, after an absence of sixteen years, their old minister still retained his hold on the affections of the people among whom he had lived and worked so long.

Outside the hall the scenes were even more impressive, and were declared by those whose memories went back for half a century to have been unparalleled in Edinburgh since the funeral of Dr. Chalmers, in 1847. Along the whole of the three miles between the Synod Hall and Echo Bank Cemetery traffic was suspended, flags were at half-mast, and all the shops were closed. As the procession, which was itself fully a mile in length, made its slow way along, the crowds which lined the pavements, filled the windows, and covered the tops of the arrested tramway cars, reverently saluted the coffin. When the gates of the University were passed, not a few thought of the time, more than fifty-seven years before, when he who was now being borne to his grave amid such great demonstrations of public homage, came up a shy, awkward country lad to begin within these walls the life of strenuous toil that had now closed. How much had passed since then! How great was the contrast between the two scenes! A little later, when the procession passed down the Dalkeith Road, everyone turned instinctively to the house in Spence Street, where he had lived his simple and godly life, unconscious that the eyes of men were upon him. As the afternoon shadows were lengthening he was laid in his grave; and many of those who stood near felt that a great blank had come into their lives, and that Scotland and the Church were the poorer for the loss of him who had followed his Master in simplicity of heart and had counted cheap those honours which the world so greatly desires.22

It is difficult to count up the gains and losses of a life. He had great gifts,—gifts of abstract thinking and writing, powers of scholarly research and continuous labour,—but his life had followed another path determined by his early choice. Was this choice a wise one? It is difficult to say. But two things seem clear. One is that he never appears to have regretted it. At the public service in the Synod Hall, Principal Rainy gave thanks for "those seventy-four years of happy life." These words are entirely true. His life was an exceptionally happy one. This surely means a great deal. If he had missed his true vocation, he could not have had this happiness.

The second noticeable point is, that his choice made the influence of his personality strong throughout Scotland. He seems to have recognised that his true home lay in the region of Christian faith and works, in the great common life of the Church; and so he made his appeal, not to the limited number of those who could read a learned theological treatise which the changing fortunes of the battle with Unbelief might soon have put out of date, but to the common heart of the whole Church. That great assemblage from all parts of the country on his funeral day was the response to this appeal, and the best answer to the question as to whether he had erred in the choice of a calling and wasted his powers. Waste there undoubtedly was. In every life this cannot but be so, for a man must limit himself; but, if it be for a high end, the renunciation will be blessed with some fruit of good. And so, although the memory and the name of John Cairns may become fainter as the years and generations pass, his influence will live on in the Christian Church, to whose ideal of goodness he brought the contribution of his character.

Footnotes

1 *Memoir of Sir W. Hamilton*, p. 231.

2 *Fragments of College and Pastoral Life*, pp. 24-25.

3 *Life and Letters*, pp. 94-95.

4 It would appear that it was not an uncommon custom in Scotland in former times to have family worship immediately after a death. Perhaps, too, this verse from the 107th Psalm was the one usually sung on such occasions. There may be a reminiscence of this, due to its author's Seceder training, in a passage in Carlyle's *Oliver Cromwell*, where, after describing the Protector's death, and the grief of his daughter Lady Fauconberg, he goes on to say, "Husht poor weeping Mary! Here is a Life-battle right nobly done. Seest thou not

'The storm is changed into a calm

At his command and will;

So that the waves that raged before,

Now quiet are and still.

Then are *they* glad, because at rest

And quiet now they be:

So to the haven he them brings,

Which they desired to see.'"

5 Afterwards author of a learned but fantastic Commentary on the Epistle to the Hebrews. Biesenthal had an enthusiastic reverence for what in the hands of others were the dry details of Hebrew Grammar. "Herr Doctor," a dense pupil once asked him, "ought there not to be a Daghesh in that Tau?" "God forbid!" was the horrified reply.

6 Some words are very hard to pronounce with a burr in one's throat. Dr. Cairns used to tell that on one occasion, long after he had got well used to the sound of the Berwick speech, he was under the belief that a man with whom he was conversing was talking about a *boy* until he discovered from the context that his theme was a *brewery*.

7 *Memoir of Sir W. Hamilton*, pp. 299-301.

8 *Macmillan's Magazine*, December 1864, p. 139.

9 *Recent British Philosophy*, pp. 265-66.

10 See above, pp. 44-45.

11 *Life and Letters*, p. 307.

12 *Fragments of College and Pastoral Life*, pp. 38-40.

13 *Life and Letters*, p. 295.

14 His eldest brother, Thomas, had died from the effects of an accident in 1856.

15 In accordance with the old Scottish custom, Dr. Cairns wore gloves during the "preliminary exercises," but took them off before beginning the sermon. On the Sunday after a funeral he discarded his Geneva gown in the forenoon, and, as a mark of respect to the deceased, wore over his swallow-tail coat the huge black silk sash which it was then customary in Berwick to send to the minister on such occasions.

16 *Life and Letters*, p. 560.

17 "All fair things be thine."

18 *Life and Letters*, p. 661.

19 In the following year (1882) he received the degree of LL.D. from Edinburgh University.

20 *Life and Letters*, p. 743.

21 *Life and Letters*, p, 769.

22 Six years later the sister who had so long lived with him was laid in the same grave. William Cairns sleeps with his kindred in Cockburnspath churchyard.

Milton Keynes UK
Ingram Content Group UK Ltd.
UKHW030626061024
449204UK00004B/288